I0147881

Make him a Sandwich

WHY REAL WOMEN DON'T NEED FAKE FEMINISM

CANDACE OWENS

PLATFORM
PRESS

PLATFORM
PRESS

Copyright © 2025 Candace Books, LLC
Published by Platform Press

All rights reserved.
No part of this book may be used or reproduced in any
manner whatsoever without permission except in the case of
brief quotations in critical articles or reviews.

ISBN: 978-1-63582-612-8 (hardcover)

10 9 8 7 6 5 4 3 2 1

FIRST EDITION

Printed in the United States of America

CONTENTS

BEWARE THE IDES OF MARCH

"Beware the Ides of March!" were the words famously uttered by William Shakespeare's fortune teller to Julius Caesar ahead of his assassination.

It was the evening of March 15, 2021, and I was about to go live as a guest on *Tucker Carlson Tonight*, the number-one cable news talk show at the time. My features on the program had gratefully become weekly installments, and I looked forward to providing commentary on cultural and political topics du jour. On this particular evening, producers had informed me that I would be asked to respond to a Grammy's performance by a rapper named Cardi B.

I had long since abandoned my ritual of viewing the annual Grammy award show. What I had recalled from my childhood as a magnanimous night of musical performance, I began to recognize in my adulthood as something other— something overtly political that had largely departed from the category of music altogether. Where once viewers were treated to the vocal and musical artistry and talents of performers like Stevie Wonder and Celine Dion, qualitatively, the culture had since been on a downward spiral.

Famed Chinese political theorist and philosopher Confucius once wrote, "If one should desire to know whether a kingdom *is well governed, if its morals are good or bad, the quality of its music will furnish* the answer."[1] Were Confucius similarly tasked, as I was, with reviewing the performance of Cardi B at the 2021 Grammy Awards, he would have deemed the United States ungovernable; morally, spiritually, and, therefore, musically, he would have declared us to be a nation in precipitous decline.

The song that Cardi chose to perform bears too graphic a title for me to put into print. Suffice it to say that it is about the condition of her lady parts as she engages in sexual affairs with men. In a most generous interpretation, the song is an ode of sorts to her vagina, which, according to its lyrics, she views as irresistible to men.

Though I had considered—as a matter of contextual accuracy—publishing the song lyrics here in full, I ultimately found myself unwilling to defile this book before the first chapter. The *least* offensive part of the song I could find is where Cardi refers to herself as a "whore" and a "certified freak." She goes on to describe how she puts on a "wig" and pretends to be another woman to make her man think "he cheatin'" before putting him "on his knees" to assert her dominance.

The song, if it can be meaningfully referred to as such, is without question a contender for the filthiest piece of musical content that has ever been produced in human history. That it was allowed to not only be produced but subsequently distributed and then further platformed on the Grammy's stage signifies terminal illness in pop culture. Rather incredulously, Cardi B (alongside featured rapper Megan Thee Stallion) mustered up the courage to deliver a performance that managed to meet the impossibly low bar of the song itself.

The Grammy's stage was designed with a life-sized, transparent stiletto. The heel of the stiletto doubled as a strip pole, which Cardi B opened her performance dancing on, more than half-naked, as counterfeit dollar bills rained from the sky. Trapped within the toe of the life-sized stiletto was a backup dancer, also dancing promiscuously as counterfeit dollar bills rained in on her.

And in the event that the da Vinci-level artistic genius of the giant stripper stiletto did not satiate the masses, Cardi B strutted herself to a second set design, this time a mega-sized purple bed—large enough to comfortably accommodate her four half-naked backup dancers, shaking their exposed derrieres to the audience so we never had to wonder if they had faces. And in case the implications of the purple bed, raunchy lyrics, plus the butt-shaking wasn't obvious, Cardi welcomed her similarly half-naked co-rapper Megan Thee Stallion onto the mega-sized bed so the two of them could shake their lady parts on top of one another in a provocative manner.

And so, when Tucker Carlson played a brief clip of the performance on his program to underscore the lunacy of a society that, as a matter of decency, cancels Dr. Seuss children's books on account of the perceived immorality of the deceased author[2] while simultaneously awarding pornography in our music and on TV screens, I chose not to hold back in my response. I began by listing all of the recently removed toys and monikers:

Dr. Seuss? Gone! Mr. Potato Head? Problematic, not enough genders available. We've [learned] that going

*through the supermarket can be a traumatizing expe-
rience; we lost Aunt Jemima last year, we lost Land o'
Lakes butter last year, we lost Uncle Ben's rice last year
because everything is so traumatizing for children to
look at. But [Cardi B's performance?] Virtually what we
were looking at last night was a lesbian sex scene being
simulated on television. And this is considered Feminist.
It's iconic, it's forward, it's progressive, it's the way the
world is going, Tucker. And if you don't see that then
you're a bigot! ... I agree with you that this feels more
sinister. This is starting to seem to me to be something
that isn't left or right—it's not even a political issue.
This seems like an overall attack on American values,
on American traditions. This is not about diversity
anymore; this is about perversity. We are celebrating
perversity in America.*[3]

I maintain that my critique of the performance had very
little to do with Cardi B personally. Rather, it represented a
broader critique and, perhaps more pertinently, a question
regarding the individuals who sit far above her: Who makes
the decision to allow a song of such a graphic, purposeless
nature to air during a show watched by millions—and why?
What exactly is the message they are they looking to further?

Under no circumstances did I anticipate that Cardi B herself might see the clip, but as the internet goes, she did and decided to respond to it on Twitter (now known as X).

"Yaaayyyyyyy WE MADE FOX NEWS GUYS! WAP WAP WAP," she wrote. "Matter of fact I'm just going to thank [Candace]. She put my performance on Fox News giving it more views [which] boosted the views on Youtube and is counting towards my streams and sales … REMEMBER GROWN PARENTS: ONLY YOU CAN MONITOR WHAT YOUR KIDS WATCH NO1 ELSE."

Offended by the idea that ultimately money justified a lack of dignity, I shot back.

"You are a cancer cell to culture," I began. "Young black girls are having their minds poisoned by what you are trying to package and sell to them as 'empowerment.' I'm one of the few who has the courage to tell you the truth." I then clarified my grievance by informing Cardi that she was "being used to encourage young women to strip themselves of dignity. Men typically treat women how they treat themselves. You know that."

And that's when things became interesting.

"And Black women should be more like you?" Cardi mused. "After all the fighting for equality and freedom, they should be submissive to a White man after years of abuse and rape, making them a sandwich while pregnant [because] in your words, 'that's what a woman should do'? Interesting." She then shared with her Twitter followers a video of me doing exactly what she accused me of: making my husband a sandwich while pregnant.

I was utterly shocked. There was no doubt she had dropped a figurative bomb, but just where and how had she uncovered this personal footage of me?

It turns out that one of her many fans had supplied her with the footage, but in the heat of the moment, and in a rush to publicly humiliate me, Cardi hadn't done her due diligence. Had she worked to source the video, she would have very quickly discovered that it was originally shared by me. Months earlier, I had shared a video of myself, barefoot, making a sandwich for my husband.

My surprise at seeing the video resurface was not due to its content, but rather due to the strange realization that Cardi had imagined I might be in any way embarrassed by it. She continued: "You have your own show and voice because women fought for years for us to be free to do what we please, NOT to be in a kitchen being submissive to a man."

I was once again stunned. She was stating that between the two of us, *I* was the one who had behaved in a shameful way publicly. That my having made a sandwich for my husband had somehow injured female progress. Perhaps more curious was her corresponding freedom with nudity.

In exactly what world is making your husband a sandwich deemed an act of humiliation? I thought.

In a feminist one, of course.

Because within the matriarchal web that has been carefully woven over the last seventy years in Western societies, standing barefoot while caring for a man (or children) has been perverted into the ultimate symbol of female oppression. The 1950's dedicated housewife has been dramatically recast as a woman in a power suit, outpacing a man on a corporate ladder. The conservative poodle skirt has been replaced with displays of nudity virtually everywhere we look. Of course, Cardi B did not create this modern, feminist world. In fact, in almost every way, she is a victim of it and an unwitting purveyor of the misery it begets.

At its best, the modern feminist movement is a failed revolution against biology that has ultimately reduced the worth of women within society. At its worst, it is the intentional Marxist deconstruction of the female—a march toward the collective misery of something other.

So it took a rather unexpected, public feud between myself and a rapper for me to realize just how quickly we were barreling toward such misery. In essence, Cardi's extraordinarily confounding defense of an utmost perverted performance inspired me to take up a fight for a truer, more divine femininity.

That is where and how this book begins.

Beware the Ides of March, indeed.

BIOLOGY

Picture the scene: A military commander, having just defeated a longstanding enemy, gains favor among the populace and comes into power. In order to maintain his newly established dictatorship, he ensures that his remaining political opponents are imprisoned or made to flee. But he realizes that these actions do not go far enough as there are still young men and boys who might grow up to challenge his authority. So what does he do to remove the threat of his rivals? Rather incredulously, he resolves to force those young men and boys to dress and act like women. This is not a fictionalized account. It is the true historical account of a sixth-century

BC military commander named Aristodemus of Cumae. The obvious question his bizarre course of action brings forth is why? Why did this mini-Mussolini believe that he could neutralize all internal threats to his empire if he feminized the sons of the city? What is it about men and masculinity in particular that he perceived to be menacing? Or, more to the point, what is it about women and femininity that he deemed to be the opposite?

SOCIOLOGY VERSUS BIOLOGY

What Aristodemus clearly acknowledged was differences between the sexes. But the theory he set out to test was whether or not social conditioning might abolish those differences. In essence, could nurture ultimately defeat nature? In a 2019 article for *American Mind*, author Spencer Klavan wrote that Aristodemus "had the boys of Cumae wear long hair and embroidered gowns; he made them listen to soft music and keep out of the sun, he starved them of adult male guidance. This was so none of them would ever grow up strong enough to stand against him (*Roman Antiquities* 7.9)."[4] In this way, Aristodemus was very much ahead of his time. "What a paranoid and oppressive autocrat did to the sons of his subjugated people, American mental health professionals now propose we do to ourselves,"[5] Klavan continued. Perhaps encouragingly for our own time, the reign of Aristodemus ended when his rivals, despite the best efforts of their ruler, eventually did muster the strength to overthrow him. In the end, biology won.

Futher exploring this inevitability, the late, renowned sociobiologist Edward O. Wilson dedicated most of his professional life to studying the evolution of social behaviors. He posited that sex at birth determines biological characteristics; that much of female and male behaviors can be understood through the lens of our different biological makeups. His view was that all animal social behavior is governed on a biological basis. As just one example, if one wonders why it seems that men are more naturally prone to promiscuity than women, Wilson points to the biological fact that women produce just four hundred eggs over a lifetime as the answer. Whereas men never cease the production of sperm over their lifetimes, women are biologically hardwired to be more selective with partners due to the natural aim of reproduction before egg production ceases.

Wilson devotes a whole chapter of his book *On Human Nature* to sex and its consequent links to social characteristics. He asserts that without human intervention when it comes to reproduction, women must invest 99.99 percent of the effort to bring an infant to term. This "investment" in biology starts with the very egg itself:

> *The human egg is eighty-five thousand times larger than the human sperm. The consequences of this gametic dimporhism ramify throughout the biology and psychology of human sex. The most important immediate result is that the female places a greater investment in each of her sex cells.*[6]

Consequently, as Wilson points out, "in theory it is more profitable for females to be coy, to hold back until they can identify males with the best genes."[7] This is a social anthropologist's way of saying "treat them mean to keep them keen," the old expression handed down by countless mothers to their daughters.

Yet for men, who release over 100 million sperm with each ejaculation, beyond that singular moment of sexual release, a physical commitment is not a biological requirement to sustain an infant's life. That is to say that men can neither carry an infant to term nor breastfeed thereafter. Women, therefore, have to "induce him to contribute to the care of the offspring."[8] Wilson argues that men (or male animals as a whole) therefore have a direct genetic advantage to inseminating as many females as possible: to multiply their number of offspring and thereby increase their chances of survival in the wild. Diversity, as Wilson notes, is a better guarantee of long-term survivability because it has a higher chance of surviving a diverse external environment, such as climate or disease.[9] Males are therefore more aggressive, seeking out competition with other males in an attempt to mate; the college bar fight over a girl by two linebackers isn't that far away from two male gorillas in the Central African Republic.

Wilson, whose chapter on this topic is worth reading independently, notes that there are male versus female physical differences that cannot be accounted for by anything but biology:

Pound for pound, [men] are stronger and quicker in most categories of sport ... Women marathoners have comparable endurance, but men are faster ... The gap cannot be attributed to a lack of incentive and training. The great women runners of East Germany and the Soviet Union are the products of nationwide recruitment and scientifically planned training programs. Yet their champions, who consistently set Olympic and world records, could not place in an average men's regional track meet.[10]

He then goes on to draw from studies observing cultures where boys and girls are raised with little to no differences and notes that even where external factors are at a minimum, the sexes differ in their natural proclivities. This analysis is later further developed by Wilson when he draws on the studies of hermaphrodites who "are genetically female but acquire varying degrees of masculine anatomy during the early stages of fetal development" because of gene mutation or artificial hormone treatment. For example, Wilson calls attention to progestins (synthetic hormones which were administered in the 1950s) that, in some cases, induced hermaphrodite anatomy. Studies of these hermaphrodite children (who were nearly always operated upon to substantiate their female organs at birth) revealed that the physical effects of the male hormones they had received earlier continued to manifest throughout their lives. The girls "had a greater interest in athletic skills, were readier to play with boys, and preferred slacks to dresses and toy guns to dolls."[11]

Of course, this natural biological difference has manifested itself across professions from ancient to new. Men are naturally more able to complete heavy physical tasks. Their muscle mass gives them an obvious advantage. Nature, therefore, provides them with a proclivity toward professional areas of physical might and competition—like the military.

Likewise, and as previously discussed, women's bodies are hardwired to nurture and care. It is basic biology that pre-determines the social aspects we observe. There is a natural reason women dominate the nursing profession; females possess a touch of tenderness and emotional connectivity that men struggle to produce.

There are even biological indicators when it comes to development. As a matter of established neurobiological fact, men and women differ in verbal communication, and "these differences are also (if not even more) present in children, both in the course of typical and pathological development."[12] Females learn to speak faster and will speak more words over their lifetime than their male counterparts. And although the academic and scientific research is compelling, we should think of it as supplementary to what is plainly obvious to us from our own observations.

Anecdotally, I gave birth to my first two children just eighteen months apart—a boy followed by a girl. My own experience confirms Wilson's conclusions. Baby girls certainly smile more than baby boys. My daughter would break into a smile at the slightest provocation; not only that, but she was much quieter and gentler in her interactions with both myself and my husband. My son (just under five years of age at the time of writing) is far more active and energetic than my daughter. His appetite for risk dwarfs that of his barely younger sister. Whether it was jumping from steps or off of couches, he preferred to learn physical lessons the hard way—typically via a newly acquired bruise to his head.

His sister, however, is risk averse. As she entered the toddler phase of climbing, she always tested furniture items for sturdiness—a gentle tap of the foot—before she would bear her full weight on them. She was careful and cautious and immediately showed a deeper interest in words and communication. My daughter began speaking just before the age of one. My son didn't begin speaking until he was almost two. His first word was *car*. Her first word had two syllables: *airplane*.

Also notable were the differences in their preferred methods of playing. When my son turned two, he craved aggression in a way I simply could not satiate; he wanted play-fights with Dad that entailed wrestling, running, and jumping. And it was even better if Dad could incorporate cars, trucks, trains, airplanes, or any other mechanical piece of toy machinery into the madness. The pace at which the two of them sprinted around the house, seemingly immune to battering into walls, was astounding. When people ask me what it's like to raise a young boy, I answer truthfully. *They wake up every day like they are in gladiator training camp.* My son's aggression was neither imagined nor nurtured. In fact, the theory about the seemingly-limitless energy of young boys has been put to the test. Researchers in Australia asked three different groups to participate in cycling tests: young boys (who were not regularly training) against twelve unfit adults and thirteen endurance athletes. The kids beat the unfit adults. They also bounced back as fast, if not faster, than the endurance athletes.[13] My husband has completed dozens of triathlons, as well as three ironmen races throughout his lifetime. He would offer that none of his past athletic feats prepared him for a couple of rounds with our two-year-old son in a playroom.

Curiously, however, although my son prefers his father for play, his desires shift entirely when he falls ill. I am, and have always been, his preferred parent in those circumstances. When my son needs nursing back to health, he innately desires a woman. Is this instinct sexist or biological? Did my husband and I foster an environment that led to this dynamic? Is it perhaps our politically conservative leanings that have made this all but an inevitability?

One person who has never been accused of being politically conservative is former pop star Lance Bass. In 2021, Lance (also an activist for gay causes) and his partner, Michael Turchin, welcomed twins via surrogacy: a boy named Alexander and a girl named Violet. Despite what I would imagine to be a drastically different environment than the one I fostered, Lance and his partner made very similar observations of their own children. Reflecting on their early days of parenting, Lance noticed that Violet was "way more opinionated and vocal" than her brother. Now toddlers, Lance describes his daughter as a "little bookworm" who loves to "read and just be chill," unlike her much more energetic twin brother. However, having been raised by two homosexual males, it would be difficult to make the argument that the children preferred a woman's touch when they needed comforting. Fortunately, no such argument needs to be made because Lance, in an interview with *Yahoo Life*, detailed how difficult the first year of parenting was for him:

> *The first year, they wouldn't give me any love. They never hugged, they never wanted to snuggle, and I was so upset about it. Because they would do that with my mom. My mom would come over, and boom, they'd snuggle with her.*[14]

This means that despite Lance's hope that he and his partner's affection might suffice, and despite mainstream culture insisting upon this plausibility, his infant children were able to recognize that something was missing. They innately knew they were being deprived of maternal care during a period when they biologically required it.

And though there are certainly exceptions to every rule, just as there are genetic defects and malformations, most parents in heterosexual relationships can confirm that differences between the sexes manifest mentally as well.

We've all been there: It's 2:15 a.m. You've just entered that second four-hour REM sleep cycle, descending into that deep sleep so desperately needed for the day ahead. But then you hear it. At first it's a gentle, muffled cry. *Nothing to worry about*, you convince yourself. *It's just the baby getting comfortable.* Then it arrives: the full-throated, unmistakable, earsplitting wail from your baby, promptly informing you that *no, covering your head with that pillow or tiptoeing over to simply readjust a pacifier isn't going to cut it.* This is their I-WANT-MILK-AND-LOVE-NOW scream! About at this point, a half-sleeping husband might attempt to justify the cry in every possible manner to avoid getting out of bed. *She'll probably calm down in a minute. It's likely just a nightmare. He's self soothing!*

In my household (at the time of writing, we have four children under the age of five), the dynamic runs the same throughout the daytime. In each of their first few months of life, should a cry break out during their time with my husband, it's a safe bet that I would immediately run interference. This is neither an agreement between us spouses nor some sort of unwritten rule. My husband and I both know instinctively that I will be able to return the baby to calm more quickly. Achieving peace as quickly as possible is always our aim. When it comes to infants and babies, Dad can certainly do it—but as rule, Mom can do it faster. The fact is that women are endowed with more patience than men, hence the aforementioned reason that even with the freedom to choose, we dominate in professions like nursing and social services. In my postpartum phase, I am best comforted when I am surrounded by other women, preferably from older generations, whom I intuitively know I can trust to guide and assist me. It takes a village to raise a child perhaps, but a tribe of women will suffice when it comes to an infant. This isn't to suggest that my husband is a terrible father. Rather, I intend only to suggest that he would make a terrible mother.

It didn't take four children for me to understand that my husband and I were being guided by underlying and inextinguishable biological differences when it came to child rearing. When we were just two months into raising our firstborn, I vividly recall taking a shower and wondering how I was ever going to get used to the physical demand of nursing in addition to all the other tasks that needed tending. *He's running out of onesies! When was his last feeding? I need to defrost some of the milk I've stored in the freezer. He needs warmer socks. Will we ever sleep again?* Suddenly, my husband walked into the room and issued a statement, "I need you to sign some documents."

Documents? In the myriad of items that were racing through my mind, signing documents was nowhere to be found. "For what?" I asked.

"For our son's college fund and life insurance," he replied.

The life insurance, he explained to me, would accrue a cash value overtime. He had also established a gift trust, which we would eventually use as a college fund due to the structure being more tax-advantageous. I was positively floored. While I had been thinking about diaper sizes and our son's minute-to-minute needs, my husband had been thinking about the rest of his life. *Why hadn't I been thinking about the rest of the life?* This is not to suggest that I am a terrible mother. Rather, I intend only to suggest that I would make a terrible father.

I remember smiling to myself in that moment, overcome by my understanding of a higher, innate perfection. It was a divine realization: There is a *yin* to the *yang*. My job is to let the *yang* yang. My husband's job is to let the *yin* yin. Appreciating our differences and seeing the comedy and beauty in them has made parenting feel like a natural dance between us. As the yin, I wanted more time at home and dreaded the idea of ever going back to work because I knew where I was needed. As the yang, my husband wanted to get on the phone and begin working on more ways to bring financial security into our home—he knew how he was needed.

The truth is that despite environmental factors that may help to accentuate or diminish our natural proclivities, differences between males and females from birth through adulthood have always been a "known known." And despite feminist attempts to effectively rinse or categorize those differences as sexist or patriarchal, the truth remains that (as E. O. Wilson underscores) anthropologically speaking, no human society in the history of mankind has ever managed to defeat biology.

FEMINISM VERSUS FEMINISM

It's important to begin with biology because it is this inexorable science the modern feminist ideology is desperately attempting to extinguish. This is because without a basic respect for dignity of the two sexes (biologically, socially, physically, etc.), one inevitably must pursue the disintegration of gender altogether.

When Aristodemus implemented his plan to feminize young men and boys, it was with an acknowledgment and deep fear of biology, a fear he desperately hoped he might assuage through environmental experimentation. He hoped that with enough cultural insistence, the men under his rule would part with their innate aggression. But what Aristodemus never did was go so far as to try to convince the men under his rule that they might actually *be* women. A concept as perverse and far-fetched as that would have to wait; it would take nearly two-and-a-half millennia, plus the demented psychiatric experiments of a pedophilic male doctor, to insist on this possibility. And it would take radicalized modern feminists to fight for his perverted theories to be widely implemented.

But what even is feminism? To whom do I refer when I describe "modern feminists"? A cursory search of the term *feminism* produces definitions that signify an ideology that aims to establish equality, both economically and politically, between the sexes. Deeper examinations reveal it to be a movement that has endured many transformations over the years, which has now been classified into four distinct waves.

The first wave arrived during the late nineteenth century in the Western Hemisphere and focused upon a clear political initiative: women's suffrage. When that decades-long battle came to a screeching halt in the early twentieth century, women began looking to extend their movement into different territories, which gave birth to a less-definable second wave of feminism.

Unlike the more missional feminism of the past, which focused on equal political and occupational opportunities for women, its successor, born in the 1960s, focused on the perceived cult of domesticity. It is during this wave when the concept of making a sandwich was problematized. Feminist writers of this era wrote with fury regarding the need for women to liberate themselves sexually (a topic we will explore in depth later) and held the patriarchy responsibile for setting the domestic expectations women were chained to.

The third wave of feminism arrived in the 1990s. With women already in the workforce and sexual liberation well underway, the leaders of this movement sought to expand their insatiable appetite for social justice to include battles of perceived racism and classism within society. Third-wave feminists developed an obsession with finding and destroying perceived social barriers—for not just women but all groups. This was about inclusiveness, which inevitably set the stage for the most radicalized form of feminism which has ever permeated society: fourth-wave feminism.

This current fourth wave of modern feminism began around 2010. Facing a dilemma as to how it could outdo the previous waves in its radicalism, the feminists of today set out to expand the mission of inclusivity. But with women, lesbians, minorities, and even homosexuals already included in their movement, leaders had to get more creative. They began turning over every social justice leaf until they found a cause unique enough to set them a part of from their predecessors. And finally, they landed upon something: transgenderism. Yes, these brilliant women decided that they would also include in their conquest men who believed deep down they were women. But in order to accomplish this, it meant that modern feminists would have to work to eradicate the concept of being a woman altogether. In order to accept that a man can wake up one day and simply decide he is a woman, the concepts of biology and gender would have to be done away with entirely.

Of course, the idea that a man can magically transform into a woman is a social, biological, and mental absurdity, made further absurd by the idea that women would, to their own detriment, promote this fiction.

Feminists of previous generations immediately recognized

the dilemma: If we erase the concept of what it means to be a woman by allowing men to simply claim they are women, wouldn't that mean we eradicated ourselves? This is the reason behind the rise of the now famous "TERF" attribution. "Trans Exclusionary Radical Feminists," aka TERFs, are those who stake a claim on the idea that to allow transgendered women into the feminist movement is to simply eradicate real women entirely.

It is important to remember that each wave of feminism was led by a very small contingent of radical women. In other words, despite not representing the viewpoint of the majority of women in society, they were able to effect sweeping social reforms. But how? Why didn't other women in society stand up to the madness of a fringe minority? Simply put: because it wasn't in their nature.

The majority of women in the world today do not agree with transgendered incursions into female spaces. But transgendered women (better referred to as men) are outwardly vicious toward any actual women who might stand in their way. That's because they are biologically male and much more willing to be aggressive to accomplish their goals. The stunning proliferation of the transgendered movement that we see today is taking place due to biological reasons. Women are *allowing* it to happen. We have discussed the female innate softness and compassion—a superpower when it comes to rearing children. But superpowers, when understood by forces of evil, can be used to further evil. Put simply, fringe feminists and pedophiles were able to appeal to the empathetic and compassionate nature of women everywhere to mass institute the perverted agenda of transgenderism.

Megyn Kelly, an incredibly accomplished American journalist, who, in 2014, was named one of *Time* magazine's 100 Most Influential People in the World, provides a stunning example of how otherwise intelligent women can be manipulated into supporting utter stupidity. In 2023, after decades of vocally supporting transgenderism, Megyn suddenly and publicly departed with the ideology in a segment on her eponymous podcast titled "Why I'm Done With Preferred Pronouns":

I was an early proponent of using preferred pronouns. As far back as the early 2000s—of saying "she" when I knew the truth was "he." It seemed harmless and I had no wish to cause offense. Trans people were tortured enough it seemed to me by nature of their dysphoria and society's disdain for them in general. So I complied. I went along with it.[15]

In other words, Megyn felt badly. Because she is biologically wired to feel compassion, she set aside the obvious fact that men cannot ever become women and supported their pursuits. She goes on in the same segment to detail how she vocally supported legislation that permitted deluded men (who think they are women) access into female bathrooms. She further notes that she even went so far as to host segments promoting the concept of transgendered children. That is, until she could no longer ignore the signs that something more nefarious was afoot:

> Teenage girls in Connecticut were losing on the track to males. Runners who had raced as male the year before then simply declared themselves female and dominated their new competitors ... Girl after girl across this country soon faced the same problem. Competing against boys who claimed they were trans was dejecting and nearly impossible. [The boys] were too strong, too big, too fast, too agile. From wingspan to femur length to lung capacity, heartsize, and musculature, they had serious advantages.

Suddenly Megyn Kelly was willing to acknowledge biology when real women began suffering the consequences of the social charade. I use her as an example not to mock her—in fact, it is always a great benefit to society when people possess the humility to admit they were wrong or acted in a way that betrayed the truth. Rather, I use her as an example because she perfectly encapsulates that despite a powerful career in corporate media (the design of earlier feminists to prove that women could be "just like men" in the workplace), Megyn still could not escape her biology. She innately wanted to care for transgendered people who were hurting (nurse complex) and felt compassion for the children who suffered from similar delusions (maternal instinct).

Now let's compare her sympathy for the insidious ideology to that of a man's.

Matt Walsh is an individual who has never been accused of being too compassionate. A top-ranking podcaster and host of the eponymous *Matt Walsh Show*, when Hollywood began glamorizing transgenderism with magazine covers and spreads, he wasted no time devoting every effort into destroying every area of its influence. This put a man named Dylan Mulvaney into his line of fire.

Dylan Mulvaney was a relatively unknown, openly gay Broadway performer who was out of work during the COVID-19 lockdowns. Likely bored, he picked up his smartphone and began documenting what he described as his "days of girlhood," which at first appeared to be a joke. Draped in a pink and red cardigan with his hair split into pigtails and while applying lip gloss, Dylan addresses his followers:

Day one of being a girl and I've already cried three times. I wrote a scathing email that I did not send. I ordered dresses online that I could not afford, and then when someone asked me how I was, I said, "I'm fine!" when I wasn't fine. How'd I do, ladies? Good? Girl power!

I remain convinced that this Instagram post was always supposed to be a hyperbolic skit. But then something Dylan couldn't have anticipated happened. Virtually overnight, he gained millions of followers, and sponsors began lining up to support him on his journey to girlhood. Within months, Dylan Mulvaney's face was everywhere. He had sponsorships with every major makeup brand (a space typically reserved for females), high-end fashion and female sports brands, as well as—quite bizarrely—tampon brands. Dylan began raking in money and fame he had never seen before, and what likely began as an act suddenly stuck. Feminists rejoiced as they had found their icon: a grown man who fantasized about living like a little girl. And they demanded he be accepted everywhere.

It was utterly perverse and not something Matt Walsh

was willing to let slide. As a father to actual little girls, Matt detested the idea that a grown man dressing up like a minor—an apparent fetish—would be so instantly welcomed and awarded in our society. He pulled no punches when he addressed the matter on his podcast, where he spoke directly to Dylan after Dylan had declared himself to be beautiful ahead of an awards ceremony:

> *You are weird and artificial, you are manufactured and lifeless, you are unearthly and eerie. You are like some kind of human deep-fake. You are a man, deprived of all the best qualities of men but without any of the best qualities of women. Even your personality is contrived; everything about you is fake. Nothing about you rings true; nobody buys the act. You'll never be accepted as a woman by anyone ... Even the people who pretend to accept you as a woman are only pretending because they are afraid of being lectured if they don't, or because they want to use you as a platform to virtue-signal. But everyone who looks at you will see something pitiable and bizarre, something utterly unfeminine in every way. You will never be able to have the identity that you are trying to appropriate, nor will you ever be able to fully escape the identity that you're fleeing. The best you can*

hope for is some sort of limbo. And yet, even in that limbo state, you will still be a man. Just not one that any of us can respect or take seriously. But other than that, champ, you're doing great.[16]

Men are biologically hardwired toward aggression, not empathy. They would never allow such nonsense to seep into their spaces. So while men wearing bad wigs and makeup have managed to replace women in sports and modeling contracts, men haven't had to suffer the same consequences. In fact, the opposite is true. When Dylan Mulvaney, still playing dress-up as a little girl, attempted to traverse into the male dominion of beer-drinking, the social backlash was as swift as it was harsh. In March 2023, while soaking in a bathtub with bubbles (as little girls do), Dylan popped open a can of Bud Light. He, of course, played up the stereotype of girls not knowing anything about sports while simultaneously promoting the upcoming college basketball season of March Madness.

It would be a gross understatement to say that men reacted poorly to Dylan being sponsored by their favorite beer.

A boycott of Bud Light, led by Matt Walsh and renowned musician Kid Rock, cost its parent company approximately $395 million dollars in US sales within a span of just four months.[17] It was a PR calamity. Men across America began uploading footage of themselves destroying their remaining Bud Light cases with guns and campfires in their backyards. Bars, liquor stores, and sports arenas alike could no longer off-load the product at events. The beer was now associated with a perversion men refused to tolerate or support. Embarrassed by the volatility and costly reaction, Dylan Mulvaney resolved to take a months-long social media hiatus. Dylan learned a valuable lesson: Men are not women. Whereas his outwardly insane behavior had been tolerated and celebrated by women who wanted to make him feel validated in his state of lunacy, men simply refused to suffer his foolishness.

It may be that more men are needed to stand up for women who are being effectively eradicated out of their own spaces by mentally ill men. Men will have to go to war on this issue, on behalf of the many women who do not, as Megyn Kelly put it, "wish to cause offense." Matt Walsh continues to provide examples of how that can be done.

In an exchange which has more than one million views on YouTube, Matt Walsh was questioned by a "trans woman" (a mentally ill young man with long hair) during a Q&A segment following a speech he gave on behalf of the Young America Foundation. The young man delivered the following point:

I have dozens of friends from diverse backgrounds: women from the Reservation, a woman from Japan, several immigrant women, I have my co-workers ... All of these people assure me, like, I'm a woman. They'll tell me, "Girl, like, there is no way you're a man." ... So the question is, how can you assert that nobody would ever see me as a woman when my material experience tells me you're wrong?[18]

Matt's answer, of course, presented a master class in illustrating the total absurdity of this debate when he calmly responded:

The fact that you have people in your life who are saying to you, "Oh, you're totally a woman," is exactly what I'm talking about. No one in my life has ever once said to me, "You're totally a man, Matt." ... If a friend of mine called me on the phone and said, "Listen, Matt, I want you to know you're really a man," I would think there was something wrong with him.[19]

He's completely correct. The very fact that there is a need to vocally affirm the subjective "realities" of trans people only works to illustrate that they are not realities at all. They are distortions that require continuous affirmation *because they are entirely fictitious.* In most cases, we only ever need to affirm the fictional realities of children, whose minds are not yet fully formed. Somehow we have now passed on this absurdity to adults who need other adults to confirm their self-imposed make-believe. The reason? Because modern feminists needed to out-radicalize their predecessors, and supporting mentally disordered men appeared to these feminists as an opportunity.

If you could choose, who would you prefer to carry you and your children out of a burning building, a man or a woman? If you were hospitalized and needed a bedside nurse to assist you throughout the day, would you prefer a man or a woman? If a traditional war of combat were to break out tomorrow, would you trust men or women on the frontlines to deliver a win? If your small children needed to be looked after in your absence, would you prefer to leave them with a group of men or women?

Biological disenfranchisement from reality is taking place, but rest assured it can only find success in the short term. Since the manifestation of fourth wave feminism and its proliferation of transgenderism post-dates E.O. Wilson's life, we may never fully know what his take would be. But we can fashion a guess based on his musings of whether or not human beings could be effectively socialized to live among other animals:

> *Human beings might self-consciously imitate such arrangements but it would be a fiction played out on a stage, would run counter to deep emotional responses and have no chance of persisting through as much as a single generation. [It] would be insanity in the literal sense. Personalities would quickly dissolve, relationships disintegrate, and reproduction cease ... Human beings could not bear to simulate the behavior of even our closest relatives among the Old World primates. If by perverse mutual agreement a human group attempted to imitate in detail the distinctive social arrangement of chimpanzees or gorillas, their effort would soon collapse and they would revert to fully human behavior.*[20]

I would argue that with enough time, this perverse social attempt to manipulate men and women into believing that, through acts of behavioral simulation, they might become one another will collapse.

Aristodemus might agree.

Because, in the end, biology always wins.

2

DEPARTMENT OF NON-EDUCATION

There is, of course, an ugly side of nature too.

Enough interaction within the animal kingdom will reveal it to you in all of its magnificent mystery. Take, for example, female bears. From birthing and feeding to hibernating with their cubs, there is no question that these creatures shoulder the load when it comes to raising their young. Contrarily, despite the biological necessity to mate with their female counterparts to reproduce, adult male bears prefer solitude; they hibernate and sleep alone. And while it is true that the males are naturally more aggressive—engaging in fights with other males to declare dominance—they often are made to face another enemy, one motivated by a purpose much grander than territorial disputes. It is the mother bear, protecting her cubs from infanticide.

Yes, a well-known and disturbing fact is that adult male bears will hunt and kill cubs—even their own offspring. The reason? Because when the mother bear is nursing, she is no longer in heat. In order to return her to mating viability, the male bear must kill the cubs. The internet is littered with videos capturing this phenomenon: the mama bear, driven by something beyond what can be meaningfully discerned from the human eye—something altogether spiritual, perhaps—will fight to her very death to protect her cubs. This "mama bear" instinct is something we will return to later on.

COLOR REVOLUTION

It has long been suspected that the United States government engages in what has come to be known as "color revolutions" around the world. A color revolution takes place when a foreign government infiltrates a nonviolent protest or movement and expands its influence in an effort to force a regime change within an adversarial country or region. The United States' role in orchestrating and staging such revolutions is a topic of immense controversy. Among other reasons, if available documentation pertaining to such events is accurate and our intelligence agencies have successfully staged revolutions overseas to expand their own power, it is worth considering whether or not they might have managed to successfully execute the same events within American borders. While we may never know for certain, it's at least interesting that at the exact historical moment the federal government began its incursion into the American education system, feminists preaching against domesticity were widely platformed, demanding that women get out of the house and into the workforce. Suddenly, the second wave of feminism was provided a new context. Much has been documented about the systematic removal of fathers from the home via government incentives. The resulting and long-lasting damage, particularly to young boys who wind up without crucial guidance, has finally become a mainstream conversation. But what has been said about the removal of mothers from their natural positions as stewards of their children's development?

In 1970, Gloria Steinem, the infamous feminist whose landmark picture I parody on the front cover of this book, published an article in *Time* magazine that became, in many ways, a manifesto for the 1970s women's movement. Steinem articulated their motives, writing that "women don't want to exchange places with men. Male chauvinists, science-fiction writers and comedians may favor that idea for its shock value, but psychologists say it is a fantasy based on ruling-class ego and guilt."[21] This is an important statement to really think about because it suggests, rather shockingly, that the aim isn't for men to take on the role of rearing children, but rather that *neither* parent should have to shoulder that responsibility. But if not Mom and Dad, then who?

Steinem offers a solution, proposing that "for parents of very young children, however, a special job category, created by government and unions, would allow such parents a shorter work day. The revolution would not take away the option of being a housewife. A woman who prefers to be her husband's housekeeper and/or hostess would receive a percentage of his pay determined by the domestic relations courts."[22] In short, the revolutionary, feminist solution to dealing with children was to expand the government. This meant calling for more taxes, more courts, and the formation of more unions. Needless to say, the federal government saw an opportunity.

When President Jimmy Carter issued his statement signing the Department of Education into law in 1979, he closed with the following remark: "I would like also to salute the active participation in this legislative struggle by a strong coalition of groups devoted to educational quality and equal educational opportunity. You refused to believe that education is a part-time responsibility, for the Federal Government or for yourselves."[23] He must have been speaking directly to the feminists of the day. I also wonder if when President Carter made these remarks, he realized the full depth of his words: *"You refused to believe that education is a part-time responsibility, for the Federal Government."* Forty-six years later, these remarks can now be taken at face value; the federal government has taken on the full-time responsibility of educating our children, and parents, busy climbing the corporate ladder, have largely been left in the dark regarding what exactly is even deemed "educational" anymore.

Of course, it wasn't President Carter who pioneered this intentional division between parents and the academia. The origins of this Manichean division can be traced far earlier to the very founding of the American school system. In his book, *The Messianic Character of American Education*, the late American philosopher R.J. Rushdoony credits what he calls the "messianic character" of American education to nineteenth-century educator Horace Mann, commonly known as the "Father of the Common Schools." In this seminal work, Rushdoony goes back to the start of the American schooling system and, despite the overtly Christian influence of educational founders such as Mann, reveals that the system was set up to be a bridge between this world and the next. It's here in these early years of formulation that we can find passages bearing a marked similarity to how modern educators perceive their mission:

> *The Common School is the institution which can receive and train up children in the elements of all good knowledge, and of culture, before they are subjected to the alienating competitions of life. This institution is the greatest discovery ever made by man; we repeat it, the Common School is the greatest discovery ever made by man.*[24]

Rushdoony, writing in the 1960s, states, "The common schools were thus the cure-all for sin and crime. Education meant moral reformation, moral virtue, knowledge cured sin."[25] It was therefore in the earliest days of the education system that we saw "education" become the new secular bible. In the same way that the Church, for centuries beforehand, used to be the administrator of classical and religious education to both clerics and laity alike, now the State, via the public or common school system, would be the new educator in the secular faith. The logical outcome of this starting point should be clear for all: the school as the replacement for the family—rather than an adherence to parents, an adherence to the State and its immediate goals. Rushdoony delivers a chillingly prophetic analysis when he writes:

> *The messianic character of education has not changed; it has only expanded its scope, and, accordingly, its claims to support, financial; and intellectual. Sex education, counselling, psychological testing, psychiatric aid, all these things are added in the abiding conviction that knowledge is not only power but moral virtue. Given these things and more, it is asserted the new society will be created. Meanwhile social disintegration grows more rapidly, for the doctrine of universal human rights ends in the mutual cancellation of rights in either social anarchy or the surrender of rights to the mass man, to the state.*[26]

These words, written sixty years ago, should make us sit up because they underscore exactly what has taken place. The broad remit of the education system has, little by little, crept into every area of our children's developing lives—so far gone that it now seeks to penetrate the heart of their innate biology. Education for the sake of education has now become the highest goal of the State. Students are pursuing university degrees out of reflex rather than rationality, degrees with very little real-world value despite the insurmountable debt acquired to achieve them. Virtue is no longer learned through family or tradition but is instead being fashioned in the classroom. There, students are treated to a constant stream of new creeds; a plethora of meaningless platitudes devoid of any substance—such as "love is love," "misinformation," "silence is violence," "Black lives matter"—have altogether replaced hard academics. Rates of mathematical and reading literacy rates have virtually collapsed as the State lowers academic standards to cover the demise. As a matter of academic fact, students are becoming dumber with every generation while convinced, through intentional emotional engineering, that they have never been brighter.

That, of course, is the State's aim: brainwashing and indoctrinating. Churning out children who have very low chances of achieving success and who lack the intellect to understand this.

Just how the State manipulates parents into allowing it to advance further into areas and topics that should be reserved for home is a marvel. There is no better illustration of this than in the 1970s with the advancement of the sex education agenda in schools. Dr. Thomas Sowell, the acclaimed Stanford professor and academic, in his book *Inside American Education* details how the advancement of the sex-ed agenda was not, as alleged at the time, in response to an increasing demand by teens or children. Instead, the agenda was advanced by academics (and I'd be willing to bet a few feminists) who pushed for sex-ed to be taught. Sowell writes:

> *The most openly promoted and most widely intro-duced non-academic program has been so-called "sex education." ... What was the situation before mas-sive, federally-funded "sex-education" programs began and how has it changed since? Teenage pregnancy was declining over a period of more than a dozen years, before so-called "sex-education" programs spread rapidly through American school in the 1970s. Teenage pregnan-cies then rose sharply, along with federal expenditures on "sex education" programs and "family planning" clinics, many located in schools.*[27]

Sowell then goes on to illustrate how pregnancies, abortions, and rates of casual sex all increased dramatically after sex edu-cation was introduced into the school system, contrary to what had been promised by advocates ahead of time. These so-called "experts" had promised that both pregnancies and abortions would decline; neither of which did.[28] Of course, once the trend had been set, it seemed all but impossible to try and reverse it.

This has proven to be a tremendously successful State strategy when it comes to wrangling control away from parents—spell out a problem that doesn't exist, find activists and faux-intellects to demand "more education" as a solution, and then refuse to backpedal when their proposed solution proves to be an abject failure. If we need an updated example, we need only look at the radical advancement of the LGBTQ+ agenda in schools. How many children or parents do we think were actually asking for this? Again, a fake academic subject of "gender studies" has been foisted on children in an attempt to advance a radical progressive ideology that ultimately renders children weaker and dumber.

Perhaps most haunting is the fact that we are now traversing into perversion and the overt sexualization of minors. Exploring the matter further, Christopher Rufo of the Manhattan Institute wrote a piece in *City Journal* tracing the genesis of the now infamous Drag Queen Story Hours that are cropping up all over the United States, wherein parents are encouraged to bring their minor children to libraries to allow cross-dressing men to read to them. Rufo traces the roots of this practice to Gayle Rubin, the lesbian activist and writer who was immersed in the 1970s BDSM San Francisco subculture. Her intellectual hero was the "father figure of the ideology, Foucault, whom Rubin relies upon for her philosophical grounding … a notorious sadomasochist who once joined scores of other prominent intellectuals to sign a petition to legalize adult-child sexual relationships in France."[29] Rubin and her later disciples, Judith Butler and Sarah Hankins, would then normalize so-called Queer Theory into something with a purpose "to subvert the system of heteronormativity, which includes childhood innocence, and reengineer childhood sexuality from the ground up."[30]

The explosion in LGBTQ+ literature, drag queens, and transgenderism among children in liberal states is therefore not some way of catering to an unmet demand from innocent children. It is clearly what any sane person has known all along: a way of radically indoctrinating children from a young age with the goal of destroying families—an ultimately Marxist effort that we will explore further in later chapters.

And there's no question that significant strides have been made. *The New York Times* reported in 2022 that "the number of young people who identify as transgender has nearly doubled in recent years, according to a new report."[31] The report in question is from UCLA, and the authors write that the number of transgender youth between the ages of thirteen and seventeen roughly doubled from 2016 to 2017.[32]

Fourth-wave feminists and federal agencies, rejoice.

At the heart of all these changes lies the removal of the mama bear.

In 1970, average female participation in the labor force stood at 43.3 percent across all age ranges; by 2000, this had risen to 60.2 percent. But the trends surrounding mothers were far more alarming. In 1970, female participation in the labor force in the key twenty-five to thirty-four age demographic stood at 45 percent, and, by 2000, it had skyrocketed to 76.3 percent, the largest absolute increase for any age group across both sexes. Likewise, in the thirty-five to forty-four age range, female participation jumped from 51.1 percent in 1970 to 77.3 percent by 2000, and there was a similar pattern in the older age bracket of forty-five to fifty-four (54.4 percent to 76.8 percent respectively).[33] These data points from the Bureau of Labor Statistics speak volumes.

Whether it's the age women historically used to have their first child (twenty-five to thirty-four) or the age brackets traditionally associated with raising children through formative years (thirty-five to forty-four), women have drastically increased their involvement in the workforce and, by proxy, lessened their involvement with their own children's lives. The cultural glorification of the stay-at-home mother is long gone. The important role of a woman as an overseer of her children's learning, diet, use of technology, and all the other associated activities has been replaced by a society (read: State) hell-bent on making a woman's day-to-day activities as close a parallel to a man's as possible.

As a result, at the same time we've witnessed this increasing participation of women in the workplace, we've also seen, in many ways, the opposite trends accelerate: the collapse in family time. In 2021, the American College of Pediatricians published a report stating that "over the past three decades, family time at the dinner table and family conversation, in general, has declined by more than 30%."[34] The same report also detailed the correlation between time spent at the family table and improved academics, improved family relationships, lower probability of obesity or addiction, and a range of other benefits. The report concludes that "when families regularly share meals together, everyone benefits."[35] None of this would be at all surprising to anyone who understands that the family unit forms the nucleus around which societies and nations are built.

In a 2008 report titled "Reclaiming the Family Table: Mealtimes and Child Health and Wellbeing" published by the Society for Research in Child Development, Reed Larson from the University of Illinois, one of the contributing authors, writes:

Societal changes, however, have created new obstacles to family meals ... Furthermore, increased rates of mothers' employment have not been matched by increases in fathers' ability and willingness to share in preparing family meals; plus more children are living with only one parent. In many families, parents are too tired at the end of the day to take on the complex task of orchestrating all the elements of an optimal family meal.[36]

Women are also now having fewer children and at a later age than before.[37] The average age a woman gave birth at for the first time in 2021 was 27.3 versus 25.6 in 2011. Furthermore, in the 1970s, women had more kids than they do now—three versus two on average—and that number is on a declining pattern. The majority of this decline happened between the 1970s and mid-1990s. Add to this that the more degrees you have, the less children you are likely to have.[38] Presumably, this is because women are happier *without* children? It turns out, no. Rather, the "the vast majority of mothers find parenting enjoyable and rewarding ... 83% of moms say that being a parent is enjoyable for them most (56%) or all of the time (27%)."[39] Motherhood, according to the same survey conducted by Pew, is "a key part of most moms' personal identity ... The vast majority of mothers

(88%) say that being a parent is the most or one of the most important aspects of who they are as a person."[40]

Modern feminism has constructed the cultural myth that motherhood and caretaking are relics of a bygone era. In the deluded mind of the modern feminist, family mealtime conjures up an image of a tiled kitchen, an A-line dress, and a neat bun tied atop a blonde, apron-wearing housewife. The reality? Family is aspirational. Reproduction is our biological purpose. We have coldly traded the spoils of motherhood for a second breadwinner. Now Mom *and* Dad are bringing home the bacon, except nobody knows how to cook it. As a result, women have ceded control of what used to be their domain, and it is arguably the most important domain in the *entire* world: the home and environment children will grow up in. It's clear the State understands this significance and has therefore fought for this domain. Why don't women do the same?

AWAKEN THE BEAR

It was Tuesday, the 28th of September, 2021. The Virginian gubernatorial race between former Democratic governor Terry McAuliffe and Republican challenger Glenn Youngkin was in its final weeks. Perhaps distracted by the typical campaign mud-slinging voters have come to expect in the lead up to the polls, McAuliffe made a critical error. Questioned in a debate as to why he vetoed legislation as governor in 2016 that would have alerted parents to the presence of sexually explicit material in schools,[41] McAuliffe stated: "[Because] I'm not going to let parents come into schools and actually take books out and make their own decision. So, yeah, I stopped the bill ... I don't think parents should be telling schools what they should teach."[42]

This seemingly throwaway remark about parental involvement in their child's education portrayed the true belief system at the heart of the modern education system. McAuliffe's comment illustrated succinctly the true ideological drive of the modern administrative state: harness children's minds to remove parental influence, transforming them into vessels of government ideology. In what can only be described as a perfect storm, his comments came in the midst of the coronavirus "era." Barred from attending classes in person, suddenly students had to take their classes from home. This meant that parents, previously third parties to the classroom setting, were suddenly able to watch in real time as their kids were forced to work through a syllabus of academic garbage. Furthermore, radical policies being pushed by local school boards came into focus; states that had implemented policies allowing teachers to recognize children's "preferred genders" without informing parents gave parents a bitter taste of the direction of travel.[43] Suddenly, parents awakened from their decades-long trance of simply trusting the government to raise their children. They began asking questions. Parental passion was reignited—and with it, a now well-established parental revolt against school boards that has ruffled many feathers within the academic establishment.

In the end, not only did Terry McAuliffe's careless rhetoric barring parents from their children's education cost him the Virginia election, but it was also there, in Loudon County, Virginia, that American mothers realized they could begin fighting back. And they started by showing up to the previously ill-attended school board meetings.

In October 2021, a mother took the microphone at a Loudoun County Public School board meeting in Ashburn, Virginia. The video went viral:

> *My children are now in private school and are thriving … We had specifically moved them out of Loudoun County Public Schools (LCPS) due to the swift and uncompromising political agenda of Superintendents Williams, Ziegler, and the school board had forced upon us. First, it was in the early spring of 2020 when my six-year-old somberly came to me and asked me if she was*

born evil because she was a white person. Something she learned in a history lesson at school. Then, you kept the schools closed for a year and a half, despite the science indicating it was safe for kids to return. Now you've covered up a rape and arrested, humiliated, and falsely accused parents of being domestic terrorists.[44]

The mother who spoke at the podium, clearly nervous and unused to public speaking, has been joined by so many others over the past few years. In a podium speech from May of the same year, a Black mother took the mic to slam the school board for teaching "critical race theory"—a State attempt to make divisive race topics central to academic curricular. She stated: "CRT is racist, it is abusive, it discriminates against one's color; let me educate you—an honest dialogue does not oppress."[45] We even had one mother, a former refugee from Maoist China, compare the indoctrination of children in Virginia to the Cultural Revolution in China that led to the death of millions upon millions.[46]

Her words, and the words of many other mothers like her, did not fall upon deaf ears.

In 2021, an insurgency took place at school boards around the nation. Of the twenty-three states that allow for school board recall efforts, ninety-two recalls were launched with

237 officials named, and, in 2022, there were fifty-three recalls with 121 officials named. Contrast these numbers with the average of twenty-two recall efforts per year held between 2006 and 2019.[47] Many of these recall efforts in 2021 and 2022 were unsuccessful, but the sharp jump in efforts by parents to replace the governance of the school system demonstrates the increase in parental interest.

Simultaneously, there has been an uptick in homeschooling. In 2016, there were an estimated 2.3 million homeschool students in grades K through 12 in the United States; by 2021, this number had grown to 3.7 million.[48] The National Home Education Research Institute also cites internal research stating that "78% of peer-reviewed studies on academic achievement show homeschool students perform statistically significantly better than those in institutional schools."[49] Of course, the very idea that parents might begin to remove the federal government from education altogether represents an existential threat to the State and its motives. In a 2020 interview with *The Harvard Gazette*, Elizabeth Bartholet, the Emeritus Professor of Law for Harvard, took aim at homeschooling parents, describing them as "extreme ideologues":

> *Other dangers are that children are simply not learning basic academic skills or learning about the most basic*

democratic values of our society ... Society may not have the chance to teach them values important to the larger community, such as tolerance of other people's views and values.[50]

The non-argument is laughable. What Bartholet and her peers fear is a loss of power, which is why it should come as no surprise that those with the most to lose from the rise in homeschooling vehemently oppose it. That they do so while willfully promoting and defending the perverse, highly sexualized climate of non-education that *actually* threatens students must require some level of psychological dissociation.

And yet, the push to mischaracterize mothers who are concerned about their own children as "radicalized" continues. In the United States, Moms for Liberty—a charity that came together to help mothers realize the power of their voice and consequentially their vote—has been labeled an extremist group by the Southern Poverty Law Center (SPLC).[51] A 2022 article published by Reuters charts the rise of Moms for Liberty (which has more than eighty thousand members in thirty-four states)[52] as having formed three federal Political Action Committees (PACs) and one Florida state PAC for electioneering.[53] The SPLC, meanwhile, says, "They really are seeking to undermine public education holistically and to divide communities."[54] Whatever that actually means.

All across the world, mama bears are awakening and responding to various crises that face their children. In the United Kingdom, the famous "Mumsnet" forum, which lays claim to more than a billion pageviews per year, routinely demonstrates mothers coming together and advocating for issues affecting parents.[55] In 2013, the two women who founded the site in 2000 were assessed as the joint seventh most powerful women in the UK.[56]

As just one example, in 2010, Mumsnet launched a campaign called "Let Girls Be Girls." The campaign aimed "to curb the premature sexualization of children, by asking retailers to commit not to sell products which play upon, emphasize or exploit their sexuality."[57] The campaign was endorsed by a UK government review program, which proposed tighter controls on sexualized products aimed at children as well as other reforms. Mumsnet addressed the issue by stating:

> *It's no secret that the worlds of entertainment and celebrity encourage girls to believe their sexual attractiveness is paramount—and many Mumsnetters were alarmed that this trend was becoming increasingly visible in products marketed at young children.*[58]

In 2013, Mumsnet launched another campaign, this time to end the egregious practice of sales representatives in maternity wards.[59] Their campaign was again successful, prompting petitions that eventually resulted in legislation being proposed to the UK Parliament, backed by eighty cross-party members.[60]

None of these examples are to be taken as a blanket endorsement of any one site or group, but rather as an illustration of what can be achieved by mothers when they unite, particularly around the issue of children. Because there is no union, government candidate, academic establishment or other that stands a chance against mothers when we come to recognize a threat to our young.

In 2011, the University of California even published a study demonstrating what they called the "mama bear" effect. The study analyzed nursing mothers, mothers who were feeding formula to newborns, and non-mothers. The report, published in the journal *Psychological Science*, concluded that "women who breast-feed are far more likely to demonstrate a 'mama bear' effect—aggressively protecting their infants and themselves—than women who bottle feed their babies or non-mothers."[61] Women, when prompted to protect their young, revert to true animalism.

Of course, the reality is that we (again) did not need

a study to confirm what everyone already knew. Women can be gentle and beautiful, but threaten our children, and something otherworldly unlocks. The old words of the song are not wrong: "The female of the species is more deadlier than the male."[62]

The maternal bond with offspring is an ironclad law of nature. Lionesses, wolves, bears, and pretty much every female mammal will risk their own life in defense of their young. "With the full time babysitting job keeping the mother bear awake, nursing mothers often lose a third or more of their body weight over winter, while non-nursing bears lose only 15 to 25 percent."[63] How many mothers can identify with the "full time babysitting job", where the seemingly endless wake-up calls for milk disturb any sleep one can hope to get in those early days? Know that these early established bonds stay between children and their mothers for the remainder of their lives. It is well known that soldiers on a battlefield, when faced with death or life-threatening injuries, always call out for their mothers. In an article written in 2014 from Eastern Ukraine during a period of conflict in the Donbas, a surgeon from the frontline, Oleksandr Zeleniuk, offered that "when soldiers are dying, they all say the same thing: they call for their mother."[64] This truth has been attested to by battlefield medics all over the world, perhaps owed to a potent cocktail of unconditional maternal love twinned with the spirit of femininity: elements of tenderness and nurturing. There is nothing on earth that can replace the natural bond between women and their children.

Fake feminism has convinced too many to turn their backs on Mother Nature. Women would do well to remember that, far from the current cultural agenda that implies otherwise, we are fulfilled as mothers. We get to cultivate the minds of those who will sustain human existence for the next thousand years and beyond. Perhaps we have become blind to the mystifying beauty of what encapsulates womanhood altogether. We have allowed unhappy women in conjunction with an ever-expanding State to make us forget that instead of being burdened by our ability to create and sustain life, we are blessed by it. As women, just the ability to give birth renders us guardians of one of life's greatest miracles: beginnings.

3

HAPPILY EVER AFTER

As the famous expression from Rabbi Kushner goes, "Nobody on their deathbed has ever said, 'I wish I had spent more time at the office!'" The message inferred is that work does not ultimately make people happy. Rather, we have come to understand that personal relationships do. Giving credence to this aphorism, a palliative nurse named Bronnie Ware published a book titled *The Top Five Regrets of the Dying*. As the title suggests, she recorded the most common regrets her patients intimated when faced with their own mortality. The second biggest regret patients expressed to her was that they wished they had not worked so hard:

This came from every male patient that I nursed. They missed their children's youth and their partner's companionship. Women also spoke of this regret. But as most were from an older generation, many of the female patients had not been breadwinners. All of the men I nursed deeply regretted spending so much of their lives on the treadmill of a work existence.[65]

What a curious observation—and one that flies in the face of the feminist manifesto, which has long insisted that more work will equate to more happiness. That's not to suggest that working makes people miserable. At the very least, it's a means to an end, and those ends can vary: status, financial wealth, academic prowess, or simply the necessity of putting food on the table.

But the feminist industrial complex routinely insists that greater career opportunities will bring about the hoped-for state of bliss women strive for. In an article written for *Harvard Business Review*, author Sylvia Ann Hewlett gives a snapshot into the mindset of the career-orientated woman:

I can't tell you how many times over the course of this research the women I interviewed apologized for "wanting it all." But it wasn't as though these women were looking for special treatment. They were quite prepared to shoulder more than their fair share of the work involved in having both career and family. So why on earth shouldn't they feel entitled to rich, multidimensional lives? At the end of the day, women simply want the choices in love and work that men take for granted.[66]

Hewlett's article is littered with illogical jumps, but it is her perpetuation of the pervasive myth that men achieve "rich, multidimensional lives" through their careers that boggles the mind. Historically, work has always been understood to be a burden that most wish to alleviate themselves from. This understanding can at first be derived within one of the oldest axioms of mankind:

To Adam [God] said, "Because you have listened to the voice of your wife and have eaten of the tree of which I commanded you, 'You shall not eat of it,' cursed is the ground because of you; in toil you shall eat of it all the days of your life; thorns and thistles it shall bring forth to you and you shall eat the plants of the field. In the sweat of your face you shall eat bread till you return to the ground, for out of it you were taken; you are dust, and to dust you shall return."[67]

We sweat from our brows so we may eat. We work so we may provide and enjoy our lives more when we are *free* from work. Why else do the French riot every time their government threatens to raise the retirement age? Why are so many in society obsessed with the fastest route to wealth? Because they wish to have freedom removed from the obligation to work. It is utterly fantastical to suggest that men work because it supplies them with a multidimensional life. As a rule, men work to provide, and traditionally, they worked to provide for their families at home. The current obsession with women finding purpose in the workplace derives itself from a misplaced belief that the typical nine-to-five existence will make them happy.

Of course, it has now been decades since women have entered the workplace—so are women, with greater access to employment opportunities, more fulfilled and happier than ever before? Let's look at some data. In a 2009 paper written for the National Bureau of Economic Research titled *The Paradox of Declining Female Happiness*, the two authors from the Wharton School deliver a fatal blow to the myth of career-induced female happiness. They write:

> By many objective measures the lives of women in the United States have improved over the past 35 years, yet

we show that measures of subjective well-being indicate that women's happiness has declined both absolutely and relative to men. The paradox of women's declining relative well-being is found across various datasets, measures of subjective well-being, and is pervasive across demographic groups and industrialized countries. Relative declines in female happiness have eroded a gender gap in happiness in which women in the 1970s typically reported higher subjective well-being than did men. These declines have continued and a new gender gap is emerging—one with higher subjective well-being for men.[68]

The report, which blows open some of the more shocking myths in the gender equity narrative and is well worth independently reading, goes on to conclude:

Happiness has shifted toward men and away from women. This shift holds across industrialized countries regardless of whether the aggregate trend in happiness for both genders is flat, rising, or falling: in all of these cases we see happiness rebalancing to reflect greater happiness for men relative to women. This finding of a decline in women's well-being relative to that of men raises questions about whether modern social constructs have made women worse off.[69]

The authors attribute this to a variety of factors, including difficulty in assessing happiness data over time, but they do state:

> *Finally, the changes brought about through the women's movement may have decreased women's happiness. The increased opportunity to succeed in many dimensions may have led to an increased likelihood of believing that one's life is not measuring up. Similarly, women may now compare their lives to a broader group, including men, and find their lives more likely to come up short in this assessment. Or women may simply find the complexity and increased pressure in their modern lives to have come at the cost of happiness.*[70]

This research substantiates my own experience throughout the decade of my twenties and the experience of the many women who, fresh out of university, are met with the reality of what it means to enter the workforce. The average experience is one in which a woman amasses a great amount of debt attending a university with the promise that an academic degree will increase her value, but instead finds herself with an entry level position at a corporation earning a salary that makes it nearly impossible to live any sort of meaningful life. Rent, food, and student loans far surpass her monthly earnings. Long hours in the office means virtually no time during the week for social activities, and even if she does find the time, it's harder to find the energy or an activity cheap enough that won't drive her further into debt.

That, in a nutshell, is how I will affectionately remember my twenties. Despite the routine feminist urgings of our university professors, work certainly did *not* make me or my girlfriends feel any happier or freer. We worked out of necessity. We worked because student loan companies called us around the clock warning of what would happen to our credit scores if we defaulted on our payments. And we defaulted anyway—because what else were we supposed to do on our $30K salaries with nearly six figures in debt? Weekends were spent binge drinking in our cramped, shared apartments before we'd head out on the town. With enough alcohol, we managed to forget our various stresses. Our struggled existences flew in the face of nearly every magazine article we read telling us the "future [was] female." We were surrounded with feminist narrative that never quite matched our reality. And that narrative has never let up.

In 2019, *The Guardian* published an article citing Paul Dolan, a professor of behavioral science, who states, "The healthiest and happiest population subgroup are women who never married or had children."[71] That was four years before the entire academic field of behavioral science was thrown into chaos by a widespread fraud scandal. Andre Spicer, executive dean of London's Bayes Business School, stated in an interview with *The Financial Times* that "there has been a large-scale replication crisis in psychology—lots of the results can't be reproduced and some of the data has found to be faked."[72] Perhaps this explains why the media glamorization of a happy corporate woman never reflected my own experience or what the more definitive data reveals.

No doubt, if women are in fact "happier" since our entry into the workplace, then data points like suicide rates would show a marked drop over the years, right? Except they don't. Female suicide in the United States has shown no dramatic change since 1950. Rather, it has marginally increased. In 1950, the female suicide rate was 5.6 deaths per 100,000 of the population. In 2019, it was 6.

Let's use another metric: alcohol consumption. While alcohol consumption should not be used as a proxy for happiness, it's safe to say that binge drinking or heavy drinking are not behaviors normally associated with balanced living.

In a study titled "Is There a Recent Epidemic of Women's Drinking? A Critical Review of National Studies" that was published in 2020 by the scientific journal *Alcoholism: Clinical and Experimental Research*, the authors demonstrate some disturbing trends. They write, "In middle-adulthood, consumption, binge drinking, and alcohol related harms are increasing, driven largely by increases among women in their 30s and 40s."[73] But wait—shouldn't women be reaching the height of their careers during those decades? And if feminist teachings hold, shouldn't they therefore be at their happiest?

Let's take another popular topic: opioids. Surely here, in the face of the drug epidemic sweeping America, women must show a decreasing trend of usage as their possibility for equal opportunity widens. Except, once again, we don't. According to the National Safety Council, "Seven out of 10 preventable opioid overdose death victims are male … However, since 1999, female opioid overdose deaths have increased at a faster pace than male deaths—1,608% increase for females versus a 1,076% for males."[74] This last statistic is significant because opioids don't have the same history so many of the other more common drugs have. They are recent, access to them has been easier, and because they are prescribed, they don't carry the same social stigma as drugs like cocaine do. This makes opioids appear safer and less risky, which is perhaps why inherently risk-averse women are the main group increasing in usage and overdose statistics. Whatever the reason, suffice it to say these women certainly are not turning to these drugs because they are leading "rich and multidimensional" lives.

Likewise, take another traditionally male-dominated industry: gambling. According to a report on *Women and Gambling Related Harm* published by BetKnowMore, which studies the UK gambling sector:

> *Over the past five years, the number of women reporting a problem has risen at more than twice the rate of men, from 2,303 in 2014/15 to 3,109 in 2019, according to figures from GamCare.*[75]

Yet again, outside of the verifiably fraudulent, non-scientific web of "behavioral science," we find no evidence that women, either in the workplace or via social habit, are becoming happier. This is in stark contrast to our previous revelation that, statistically speaking, an overwhelming majority of women who choose motherhood as a full-time role find it to be fulfilling.

So why are we culturally painting the opposite picture?

MEASURING DESIRE AND SUCCESS

Of course, there are at our disposal any number of useful feminist excuses as to *why* women are unhappy in work. *Because of men!* Men keep women oppressed—not least, of course, via the specter of the gender wage gap. This menacing sword of Damocles that hangs over women, insisting that for no reason beyond anatomy, women are paid less than men. Were this true, one might imagine that all employers would exclusively hire females. Presumably, if there exists a reliably cheaper workforce, wouldn't any shrewd businessman seek to acquire it?

This doesn't happen because the oft-spoken "gender pay gap" does not exist. It is pure feminist fiction. There are so many concrete economic reports refuting the gender wage gap that any person still peddling this talking point can be instantly dismissed as unserious. As Christina Hoff Sommers writes in *Time*:

> *The bottom line: the 23 percent gender pay gap is simply the difference between the average earnings of all men and women working full time. It does not account for differences in occupations, positions, education, job tenure or hours worked per week. When such relevant*

factors are considered, the wage gap narrows to the point of vanishing."[76]

Simply put, women make different life choices than men. As just one example, CEOs and secretaries are not paid the same because they are not the same roles; they do not carry the same responsibilities or work the same hours.

The gender pay gap has been used by the feminist lobby to force employers to disclose wage data, which they believe proves there is sex-based discrimination. Instead, the data reveals how vapid their arguments are. Ironically, the more any person looks into the alleged disparity between men and women in terms of payment at work, the closer he or she will come to fully dismantling the feminist doctrine that there are no differences between the sexes.

Because what the data surrounding gender pay reveals is that even with every opportunity available to them, women do not choose the same careers as men. This point was well illustrated in the now-famous interview between journalist Cathy Newman and psychologist Dr. Jordan Peterson. In a thirty-minute discussion, which has since garnered over 45 million views, Peterson at first outlines the facts that women are generally more agreeable than men, often less assertive, and therefore less likely to ask for a pay raise as a few of the multivariate reasons women and men have variable pay. Peterson and Newman soon begin to clash, however, when Newman rebuts with an onslaught of feminist talking points:

> *Newman: Why would there only be seven women running FTSE 100 [the UK equivalent of the S&P 500] companies in the UK? Why would there still be a pay gap which we've discussed? Why are women at the BBC saying that they're getting paid illegally less than the men to do the same job? That's not fair, is it?*
>
> *Peterson: Well, let's go to the first question. They both are complicated questions. Seven women, repeat that one, there's ...*
>
> *Newman: Seven women running the top FTSE 100 companies in the UK. I mean, that's not fair.*
>
> *Peterson: Well, the first question might be ... why would you want to do that?*
>
> *Newman: Why would a man want to do it? It's a lot of money, it's an interesting job ...*
>
> *Peterson: There's a certain number of men, although not that many, who are perfectly willing to sacrifice virtually all of their life to the pursuit of a high-end career. So they'll work ... These are men that are very intelligent; they're usually very, very conscientious; they're*

*very driven; they're very high-energy; they're very healthy;
and they're willing to work seventy or eighty hours a
week, non-stop, specialized at one thing to get to the top.*

*Newman: So you think women are just more sensible.
They don't want that because it's not a nice level.*

*Peterson: I'm saying that's part of it, definitely. And so
I worked ...*

*Newman: So you don't think there are barriers in their way
that prevent them getting to the top of those companies?*

*Peterson: There are some barriers, yeah, like ... men for
example, I mean, to get to the top of any organization
is an incredibly competitive enterprise and the men
that you're competing with are simply not going to roll
over and say, "Please take the position." It's absolutely
all-out warfare.*[77]

Their conversation is significant as it diligently underscores
nearly everything that is wrong with the women's movement.
Feminists like Newman insist on the equality of outcome
without ever pausing to consider whether the outcome is even
desirable. Does working eighty-hour weeks sound like happiness? Then why on earth are women highlighting that statistic
as evidence of anything more than female sensibility? This is
the travesty of modern feminism. It seeks to mimic even the

miseries of men in its quest for equality. I'm convinced that, given enough time, feminists will notice that just 10 percent of the prison population in the United States is female. They will then kick up a fuss about sexism, call it the "gender crime gap" and begin a quest to erase these statistical differences without ever pausing to consider whether or not increasing our numbers among serial killers will actually render us happier.

Given everything we now know about the career choices men and women make, and the fact that men are more likely to pursue career over family due to basic biological differences, it should come as no surprise that the top ten wealthiest people in the world are men. More interesting, however, is the world's top wealthiest women.

According to *Forbes*, the world's three wealthiest woman are Alice Walton, Francoise Bettencourt Meyers of the L'Oreal fortune, and Julia Koch. Alice Walton is worth $101B. She is the only daughter of Walmart founder Sam Walton. Bettencourt Meyers is worth $81B as of 2025. She inherited her wealth from her mother, who inherited it from her grandfather, who founded the company. Then comes Julia Koch of Koch Industries, worth a similarly mind-blowing $74B. She also inherited her wealth from her late husband, David Koch. See a trend?[78]

As of 2025, of the thirty top wealthiest women in the

world, only three women haven't come into their wealth via birthright, divorce, or having been made a widow. Of those three women, two of them co-founded businesses with their husbands. That leaves just one woman on the list who earned her wealth solely.

There is, of course, absolutely no issue with inheriting wealth via marriage or otherwise. We work hard in life with the hope that our offspring or those we love will benefit. Nonetheless, it is indeed interesting that virtually none of the world's most financially successful women are those who have gone out and pioneered a business on their own. Certainly, women have been in the workforce long enough to have done so, were that their desire.

Quite opposingly, if we look at the top ten male billionaires, *all* of them are self-made. The list includes billionaires who are young and have made their fortunes in the last twenty years, like Jeff Bezos and Elon Musk. Indeed, it's actually quite interesting that out of the thirty wealthiest people in the world, the *only* people to have inherited wealth are women (with the exception of the Walton family brothers).

You are now probably in deep wonder about who the exceptional, singular self-made woman is on the list. You likely have never even heard of her, which is curious. Her name is Zhou Qunfei. She is the Chinese founder and chairman of Lens Technology. She was a migrant factory worker who took the plunge to be an entrepreneur in 1993 before listing her company on the Shenzhen Stock Exchange in 2015. Interestingly, despite the extremely well-enforced "One Child Policy" implemented in China between 1979 and 2015, Qunfei, who was born in 1970, has two children.[79]

Despite her incredible wealth and inspiring story, if you asked the average person, they would have more than likely never heard of her. In remarkable contrast, if you asked that same person who the most successful, self-made men in the world are—chances are they will name at least two or three in the top ten: Elon Musk, Jeff Bezos, Bill Gates, Carlos Slim, Michael Bloomberg, Warren Buffet. Their names are some of the most recognized in the world. Why? Feminists (who similarly would not have been able to name Zhou Qunfei) would likely attribute it to another example of sexism.

Thoughtless. Tired. Untrue.

What it actually reveals is that women hold entirely different views than men regarding success. We simply do not equate it to wealth. It is male interest in financial success of men like Bezos and Musk that has turned them into household names. It is an utter lack of female interest in the financial success of Qunfei that has rendered her unrecognizable. Rather, if you asked women who they thought the most successful women in the world were, you'd likely hear names like Oprah, Taylor Swift, or Beyonce. All of them are global celebrities who have achieved commercial success but register nowhere near the same metric of wealth of the men we've discussed.

Most would agree that Taylor Swift is at least as famous (if not more) than Jeff Bezos. Jeff Bezos certainly has much more money. An interesting question to consider is what does Taylor Swift have more of? What do all these celebrity women have more of than those wealthier men? I would argue it's influence. It seems women measure success in terms of cultural influence, not bank accounts. And it must be pointed out that these women earned their success in ways that only further substantiates that there are biologically driven, innate traits of women.

More simply put, women achieve power by shaping industries that we inherently understand.

Oprah is a brilliant communicator who managed to spin that talent into a television and broadcast empire so successful that there is now a psychological investment pattern called "The Oprah Effect," which has since been turned into its own TV series. Oprah came from poverty. She exploited female empathy and compassion and struck television gold. Famed for *The Oprah Winfrey Show*, she platformed sob stories, further drawing on the emotion of her audiences.

And who can question the superstardom success of Taylor Swift? Millions of little girls and adult women adore her around the world. But she, too, mined compassion and empathy, churning out hit song after hit song regarding the heartache she experiences falling in and out of love.

It seems the most recognized women in the world have earned their success through the magnification of empathy and compassion. In pursuit of "gender equality," we have done little more than prove gender differences. We have proven that women are better at communication, emotional understanding, and beauty—which is why we dominate in fields like fashion, marketing, nursing, and teaching. And when left to decide upon our own interests, we simply do not find the traditional male metrics of financial power as inspiring as men do.

We have also proven that men are better at being traders, money managers, and disagreeable Fortune 500 CEOs. Modern-day capitalism is the more civilized version of male warfare. Instead of cutting off one another's heads in battle and raiding another tribe's resources, we have corporate M&A, equity and debt capital markets, and boardroom coups.

The irony is that "gender diversity" (one of the explicit

aims of modern feminism) will never be achieved by asking women to behave like men. Rather, gender diversity is immediately achieved by recognizing that men and women will always be different.

The women's movement has successfully convinced women that they need to enter this harsh battlefield. The result has been that women have all-too-willingly swapped the traditional aims of homemaking and motherhood with a flawed belief that it will render them happier. The idea that to achieve "rich, multidimensional lives," women *have* to aspire to lead Fortune 500 companies is a pseudo-intellectual lie born from a pseudo-intellectual movement.

Evidentially, women today compared with women of yesteryear are not happier by any meaningful metric, so perhaps it's time to pause and fully consider why that may be. If the grass is not in fact greener on the other side, perhaps we should stop insisting that it is.

There is no greater fulfillment found in this mortal life beyond children and family. It seems that even men on their deathbeds agree. "I wish I spent more time in the office," said nobody, ever, in their final moments.

There is no "boss-girl" that will prove an exception to that rule.

4

BEYOND THE PALE

When I was eleven years old, I joined the drama club at my school. For our annual musical, we performed *Fiddler on the Roof*, based on a series of stories collectively titled *Tevye and His Daughters*. As it was my first year in middle school, I was delighted that, after rounds of auditions, I was cast as one of Tevye's daughters. The fictional story depicts the life of an impoverished Jewish man, his wife, and his five daughters living in a village outside of imperial Russia at the end of the nineteenth century. They lived in what is historically known as the "Pale of Settlement," an area that encompasses parts of modern-day Belarus, Ukraine, Poland, and Lithuania. Tevye is a faithful, traditional man who is looking to marry off his three eldest daughters to decent men. But it turn out his daughters have different plans. Seeking to flout traditions, they fall in love with men who do not meet his approval. Despite having her marriage arranged by her father to a wealthier man, Tevye's eldest daughter resists and instead marries a poor man whom she loves. Tevye's second daughter falls in love with a Marxist revolutionary who winds up arrested and eventually exiled. She chooses to follow him out of love. And his third daughter, Chava, secretly elopes with a non-Jew and leaves her close-knit family to begin a life with him in Poland.

Ultimately, it is a story about a changing world—women bravely breaking with traditions to pursue the futures they want rather than futures dictated to them by oppressive norms.

To be honest, I thought the musical was quite boring … until decades later when I realized that the real story of the young women who lived in this historical settlement is far more chilling and, indeed, much stranger than fiction.

FEMINIST BEGINNINGS

The following is a true account.

Born into a religious family, Gesia Gelfman was only a teenager when her father chose a husband for her, whom she referred to as a "Talmudist." On the eve of her wedding in 1868, she ran away, attributing her distress to "repulsive rituals dictated by ancient Jewish customs." Thereafter, she wound up in the city of Kyiv, where she became an active member of several socialist clubs. These socialist clubs were committed to a Marxist belief that in order for the working class to achieve true economic justice, they would have to overthrow the emperor of Russia and bring in radical, progressive change. Gelfman joined the propagandist movement, helping to distribute socialist propaganda throughout the empire. Despite being arrested and charged with fomenting unrest throughout the Russian empire, Gelfman emerged from prison even more radicalized. She joined a militant party known as The People's Will, which held the position that violence was needed to achieve their Marxist goal. They at first tried to blow up the emperor's train, but their plot went sideways. Nevertheless, on March 1, 1881, they would achieve their goals. Having prepared dynamite grenades, Gesia Gelfman and five other activists assassinated Czar Alexander II.

Sophia Perovskaya was Gesia's peer and accomplice in the planned assassination. History recalls her as the leader of their revolutionary organization, Narodnaya Volya, which translates to the "People's Will." It's curious given the fact that Sophia's wealthy upbringing would not have provided her with any worker experience. Sophia was brought up as an aristocrat. Her family owned a vineyard in Crimea. Her father, Lev Perovsky, was the military governor of St. Petersburg. It should be said that the members of Narodnaya Volya attempted to assassinate the Czar multiple times, and each time, until their success, the highly educated and well-to-do Perovskaya helped prepare the dynamite bombs.

On March 1, 1881, Czar Alexander II was traveling through St. Petersburg by horse and carriage after watching the military roll call. Unbeknownst to him, Sophia Perovskaya was blowing her nose into a handkerchief nearby, a preplanned signal to two awaiting assassins that the Czar's carriage was approaching. Soon thereafter, a nineteen-year-old student named Nikolai Rysakov stepped out in front of the carriage, carrying a parcel. The parcel detonated, killing one of the guards, but sparing the Czar. Unfortunately, the czar then emerged from his carriage, allowing for a second attacker—also a student, named Ignacy Hryniewiecki—to appear with a bomb strapped to his chest. He detonated some mere feet away from the Czar, killing both himself and his target.

The Czar's horrific assassination is viewed by historians as one of the first recorded suicide bombings. Narodnaya Volya is deemed the world's first organized terrorist group, which makes their demographics worth exploring:

At the time People's Will struck the participation of women in Russia's revolutionary movement was far from novel. Indeed, the 1878 attempts by two women who had become radicalised at university reading groups— Vera Zasulich and Maria Kolenkina—to assassinate the governor of St Petersburg and a state prosecutor inspired the founders of People's Will. Like Zasulich and Kolenkina, the women who were central to creating this new terrorist organization—Sophia Perovskaya and Vera Figner—were products of an era of hope and fracture in the land of the Tsars. Whilst the peasant population of the countryside had remained socially stagnant and bound to their landlords for generations, in the cities a liberal-minded intelligentsia grew in voice and ambition, fuelled by socialist and Jacobin theories from Europe, and the home-grown ideology of nihilist populism. It was with proponents of these radical ideologies that Figner and Perovskaya mixed in their late teens, finding a sense of belonging and purpose. Both women were born to noble parents, educated and dedicated to the betterment of Russian society. Moreover, in keeping with the trends in reformist thought, Perovskaya and Figner were accepted by their fellow male radicals as equals in the revolutionary struggle.[80]

The bloody anarchist movement and the world's first organized terrorist group were comprised by the intelligentsia. And, surprisingly, a large number of women.

Luckily, we do possess meticulous numbers on The People's Will, a notorious radical organization from the 1870s and 1880s. These figures reveal that Jewish women were spectacularly overrepresented in this circle. The People's Will attracted 2193 activists during the decade of the eighties. Among these two thousand some radicals were 95 Jewish women, who represented almost a third of the 348 women in the party ... Moreover, the 95 Jewish women were twice as well represented among the Jewish activists as Christian women were among the Christian activists.[81]

The reason for the over-representation of Jewish women should not be construed in any way to suggest that it was a tenet of Judaism, but rather a sign of the unfortunate times in which Jewish people were restricted and oppressed within an empire. Of course, any minority group that is subjected to systemic oppression will become keen to start a revolution. The purpose of exploring this particular group is that they represent the earliest formation of what can be termed a feminist movement in human history.

And it was deadly.

Sophia Perovskaya was apprehended nine days after the assassination. She would become known as Russia's first female terrorist. On April 15, 1881, she and her accomplices were marched through the streets of St. Petersburg, dressed in black prison garb, with "czaricide" written on placards draped around their necks. Angry mobs lined the streets, shouting at the condemned murderers. According to accounts, Sophia maintained her composure until just before she was hung.

Gesia Gelfman (whose apartment was used as a safe house to make and store the grenades) was raided the day after the czar's assassination. She avoided a public hanging due to her condition at the time of arrest: she was pregnant. Far from the future her parents had planned for her within the Pale of Settlement, Gesia had fallen in love with a noble radical named Nicolai Kolotokevitch. He, too, had been captured and hung alongside Sophia Perovskaya for his role in the plot against the Czar. With the father of her child executed, Gesia gave birth to their daughter in prison. The infant was then sent to an orphanage, where she soon died. Gesia died five days thereafter from peritonitis. It was a dramatic ending for a young woman who had defied her parents and the beginning of what would come to be defined as Jewish pogroms throughout Russia. When people learned of her role in the assassination, "several marauding hooligans who plundered Jewish villages in the pogroms of 1881 targeted her as the *Jewish* killer of the Czar. Of late historians have vigorously debated the complex causation of the pogroms which began that spring of 1881, largely refuting the myth that government officials provoked the attacks. What is not disputed is that citizen hooligans in Kiev 'made Gelfman into the symbol of all of the Jews.'"[82]

This, of course, was unfair. What was happening within the Jewish community was a generational divide in thought. While some radicals may have agreed with Gelfman, many more did not and were therefore undeserving of the violence being enacted against them in retribution. In other words, it was a mixed bag. What should be understood, though, is that following this episode, a large number of Jewish families emigrated out of Russia. Many of them wound up in the United States. According to calculations in the *American Jewish Yearbook*, 5,692 Jewish immigrants arrived in New York in 1881. Thousands more would depart for America in 1882. And while the majority of these individuals had been wrongly persecuted on behalf of the crimes committed by a radicalized few, there were, of course, some committed anarchists among them.

Most of the radicals from Russia were former students or graduates of the gymnazium [Russian and Polish secondary schools]. A good number of those educated young people came from Lithuania. But the vast majority came from South Russia right after the pogroms that took place in a number of Russian cities. Most of those educated people were quite young and there were only a few middle-aged or elderly people among them. A number of them had belonged to a variety of secret revolutionary circles in Russia and a few of them had even belonged to that famous revolutionary party, Narodnaya volya. Others only sympathized with revolutionary or Socialist movements, but many were already familiar with Socialist literature from their country of origin.[83]

One such radical who settled in New York was a revolutionary named Emma Goldman. When the czar was assassinated, she was only twelve years old and living in the German city of Konisberg with her mother, Taube. Taube was devastated by the news and wanted the assassins brought to justice. But Emma was inspired by the radicals. "In the years to come, Emma's resentment of her father's attempts to control her behavior and of the Judaism she associated with her father would fuel her anarchist politics." This again reveals that the murderous politics did not reflect the Jewish faith whatsoever, but rather an adolescent struggle turned deadly due to the repressive state of things.

AMERICAN FEMINISM

When people think of the early feminist movement in America, they likely associate it with Margaret Sanger, the woman who dedicated her life as an advocate of birth control and sex education. It was Margaret Sanger who opened the first birth control clinic, which would eventually evolve into the Planned Parenthood Federation of America. In addition to this, Sanger was deemed one of the most influential advocates for the suffrage movement. What most are not aware of, however, is that Margaret Sanger's mentor was Emma Goldman, who can only be described as an utter psychopath.

In fact, I would argue that the single most violent contributor to the death and destruction of America in the twentieth century was Emma Goldman. There should be entire courses in psychology dedicated to exploring her psychopathic tendencies. So as not to get lost, I will summarize her contributions.

As previously mentioned, Emma was born in 1869 within the Russian Empire (Lithuania), and emigrated to the United States alongside her sister in 1885 at the age of sixteen following the pogroms. She, too, considered anarchy as a symbol of her education. And she sought to seed and fertilize that philosophy throughout America to devastating effect.

Goldman demonstrated an understanding of what made the women of Narodnaya Volya so very effective against all odds: a theory of "propaganda of the deed." Better understood, a theory that, via works, you could inspire panic among the masses and convince them to violently revolt against real (or imagined) authority.

In 1886, just one year after Emma emigrated, the United States saw its first ever terrorist attack and bombing. It began with a labor rally in Chicago ostensibly organized by workers who were striking for an eight-hour workday. As police were working to disperse the crowd, suddenly a person threw a dynamite bomb toward them. Seven anarchists were found guilty of coordinating the bombing, and notably, only one of the seven was an American. Five of them were recent immigrants from Germany, while another had emigrated from England. Rather mysteriously, the person who was suspected of throwing the bomb never faced any charges because after being questioned twice by police, he managed to flee and was never recaptured. His name was Rudolf Schnaubelt, and he was also a recent immigrant from Bohemia.

> *There never has been any doubt in Chicago police circles that it was Schnaubelt who threw the bomb. All the evidence pointed to him as the chief tool of the leading conspirators, and it has never been controverted or strongly denied. The testimony on the trial, summed up, went to show that Lingg made the bomb, that Spies lighted the fuse with a match while standing in the alley opening on the Haymarket square, and that Schnaubelt threw the bomb into the ranks of the police.* [84]

Curiously, rather than feeling fearful that a terrorist attack had taken place in her new country, Emma Goldman felt inspired. She viewed the accused immigrants (four of whom were eventually tried and hanged) to be martyrs. According to Emma, this only furthered her consumption of anarchist principles, and in her words, she "sent for the literature advertised in the paper and [she] devoured every line on anarchism

[she] could get, every word about the men, their lives, their work. [Emma] read about their heroic stand while on trial and their marvelous defence. [She] saw a new world opening before [her]."[85] Emma was apparently so excited by the Haymarket affair that upon her death, Emma Goldman made the decision to be buried in the same cemetery in Chicago as the men who were convicted for the bombing. In other words, it was her dream to be reunited with other "martyrs" in the afterlife.

It's well known that Goldman enjoyed a decades-long relationship with a man named Alexander Berkman (formerly Ovsei Osipovich Berkman). Like Emma, Ovsei Berkman was born to a Lithuanian-Jewish family within the Russian Empire's Pale of Settlement. With restrictions eased on Jews under Alexander II, he and his wealthy family eventually moved to St. Petersburg. He, too, was well-educated at a *gymnazium* and enjoyed a carefree life with servants in his childhood. Immigrating to the United States in 1888, Berkman, rather curiously, instantly joined the Pioneers of Liberty, the first Jewish anarchist organization in the United States, which would later become the Knights of Liberty. The group attracted like-minded young militants and was organized around the Haymarket bombing trials. Similar to Narodnaya Volya, they published propaganda in a Yiddish-language newspaper, *Varyhayt*, and later, *Freie Arbeiter Stimme*. And similar to

Narodnaya Volya, the group was explicitly anti-religious—again signifying that the radical philosophies were not an aspect of Judaic faith.

Emma Goldman met Berkman through the Pioneers of Liberty when a mutual friend and member of the organization, Hillel Solotaroff, introduced the two at Schwab & Sach's café in New York.[86] The café was an attraction for Eastern European Jewish immigrants and was established by immigrant and eventual anarchist Justus Schwab.[87] This meeting would spell future disaster throughout the world.

In July 1892, the duo attended the Homestead strike in Pennsylvania at a factory that was owned by American industrialist Andrew Carnegie and run by his partner Henry Frick. At the heart of the issue were increasingly radical demands the union workers were making that Frick and Carnegie felt ran counter to productivity. Frick was happy to allow the union contract to expire and to instead hire non-unionized workers. Further signifying his commitment, he locked the workers out of the factory and hired police to protect the premises. He could have never imagined that this action would lead to death. History is indecisive on which side fired first, but I have an idea. The end result of the day was that two workers, as well as two security guards who were protecting the factory, were killed.

This tragedy worked only to further Henry Frick's resolution not to renew the contracts of a workforce that he and many others deemed to be radicalized. On July 23, 1892, Frick was walking back to his office when Alexander Berkman, armed with a gun and a dagger, shot him four times and stabbed him. Fortunately, Frick survived the attack. Police raided the apartment of Emma Goldman, as they suspected she too was implicated. The press begin to refer to her as the "Queen of Anarchy."

And they were correct. Emma's name would seemingly continue to surface every time an unimaginable act of violence occurred.

For instance, in 1901, American President William McKinley was shot twice during a public speaking event in New York. Unable to recover from his injuries, the president died eight days later. Leon Czolgosz was the man who pulled the trigger. After his arrest, he told authorities that he had been inspired to commit the act upon hearing a lecture from Emma Goldman. Once again, authorities arrested Emma as well as other anarchists in her circle. But after two weeks, and without any direct evidence linking Emma to the attack, she was released.

Then there was the mysterious case of Gaetano Bresci. Born in Italy, he immigrated to New York City in 1897.

He lived in New York City for some time and also visited Schwab & Sachs café, the hub of anarchy that Emma used as her mailing address. One day, Bresci departed back to Italy. Shortly thereafter, on July 29, 1900, Bresci assassinated King Umberto I of Italy, shooting him three times.

His act didn't seem to startle Emma Goldman. Because as we've learned, acts of violence—or "propaganda of the deed"—were deemed as a necessary means to a perceived end. She eulogized Gaetano many times in the press thereafter.

So what is left for a female anarchist to do other than to declare herself a fighter for women and mentor other women in her psychopathic ways?

In 1910, a young woman named Margaret Sanger moved to New York City, having grown bored of life in the suburbs. That same year, she met Emma Goldman.

It was a match made in hell.

BIRTH CONTROL PROPAGANDA

It was Goldman, not Margaret Sanger, who began the birth control movement in America. In researching Margaret Sanger, biographer Vivian Gormick was surprised to see how Goldman's name had been effectively rinsed from the movement:

Goldman had been lecturing about family planning and women's sexual freedom long before Sanger came to New York. In fact, when Sanger launched "The Woman Rebel," a monthly newsletter promoting contraception, she used the famous anarchist phrase, "No Gods! No Masters!" as the slogan for her publication ... When I began my research, I was shocked to see how completely separate Goldman's name had become detached from the birth control movement. Who knew that Sanger had published articles in "Mother Earth," Goldman's anarchist magazine? [88]

Indeed, the revisionist history as it pertains to the birth control movement is something I too have found to be quite strange. Most women in America today are not only unaware of the origin story of the medicine they deem so critical to freedom, but they also are entirely clueless as to the openly evil agenda—which was about sterilizing women who were deemed unfit to reproduce.

Margaret Sanger was an avowed eugenicist. She wrote extensively about her aims to help move humanity forward by ensuring that people who were "undesirable" to the human race would be unable to procreate. She must have assumed that the people she targeted for sterilization were not of enough intellect to access the many articles she wrote to that psychopathic effect. In an article she published in 1923 titled "A Better Race Through Birth Control" in *The Thinker* magazine, she laid out her concerns clearly:

> *The most important problem, barring none, that confronts humanity today is that of race culture. It has often been said, and never with more truth than at the present time, that man breeds his cattle with more intelligence and care than he breeds his own kind. The draft figures alone should be sufficient to galvanize the human race to action, for the intelligence tests made on our soldiers during the recent war indicated that approximately 25 per cent of our population never attains a mentality superior to that of a twelve-year-old child. When we consider that the mentally deficient reproduce more rapidly than those of normal intelligence, we may well look into the future with dismay. Unless a halt is called, and that speedily, our race is doomed to inevitable deterioration.*[89]

Her explicit aims were to accomplish "the gradual suppression, elimination and eventual extinction, of defective stocks—those human weeds which threaten the blooming of the finest flowers of American civilization."[90]

Of course, Sanger must have understood that putting forth such psychopathic aims would not convince the target population to follow her. Her mentor Emma would have explained to her that people must be led by other means. For birth control to become mainstream, Margaret Sanger would have to create propaganda about the deed. Margaret Sanger communicated this understanding in a piece titled "The Eugenic Value of Birth Control Propaganda."

> *Birth Control propaganda is thus the entering wedge for the Eugenic educator. In answering the needs of these thousands upon thousands of submerged mothers, it is possible to use this interest as the foundation for education in prophylaxis, sexual hygiene, and infant welfare. The potential mother is to be shown that maternity need not be slavery but the most effective avenue toward self-development and self-realization. Upon this basis only may we improve the quality of the race.*[91]

Accordingly, in June 1916, Margaret Sanger was arrested for distributing pamphlets that promoted birth control to women. Emma Goldman was arrested in 1915, and then arrested and imprisoned in 1916 for lecturing and distributing material in support of birth control. We can imagine, based on the conversation today, that the pamphlets were likely aimed at motivating women through the perception of their own enslavement. *Reproductive freedom! Anarchy to overthrow nature!* This time, it wasn't a czar in Russia or a factory owner who needed to be killed—it was the very potential for life itself. The public call to action was for women to free themselves from the concept of family altogether. The private call to action was to convince women who were deemed racially or intellectually undesirable not to have children.

It should be noted that the suffragettes (most notably Susan B. Anthony) did NOT support birth control or abortion. Margaret Sanger was involved in a fringe but powerful and well-funded network of far-left publications. Sanger also claimed to have been mentored by a woman named Rose Pesotta—another immigrant from Russia's Pale of Settlement who was explicitly involved in the radical underground before choosing to immigrate to the United States.[92] Having spent a considerable amount of time researching the horrific genesis of the birth control movement, I have come to the conclusion that Margaret Sanger, today hailed as an icon of feminism, was little more than a tool of Russian Marxists looking for a new home for their deadly ideas. Sanger then was their chosen social engineer meant to drive a wedge between women and their natural inclination for family.

By that measure alone, she was exceedingly successful.

5

UGLY, NAKED, AND AFRAID

In contemporary economics, "schools of thought" are commonplace. Most well-known is the "Austrian school" whose followers believe that a free-market system mirrors universal law and is therefore best implemented throughout society. In essence, the less government intervention, the better for humanity. Standing diametrically opposed to these principles are the followers of what has come to be known as "Keynesian" theory. This was named after twentieth-century economist John Maynard Keynes who believed that government involvement could produce the best economic outcomes in a society.

I would posit that within the modern sphere of feminism, two similarly rivaling schools of thought have emerged: the Dunham Theory of Ugly and the Kardashian Theory of Plastic. Contemporary culture has boiled down the essence of what it means to be a woman between these two tabloid illustrations. It would appear that long gone are the days of Grace Kelly and classical, understated beauty. Now, only vulgarity and nudity win the day.

THE DUNHAM SCHOOL OF FEMINISM

Without question, one of the most crucial contributors to modern feminist culture is a young woman by the name of Lena Dunham. Dunham was born in New York City in 1986 to two artistic parents, a painter and a photographer. In 2008, she graduated from Oberlin College with a degree in creative writing. She subsequently became a writer and actress who rose to moderate television stardom for creating an HBO series titled *Girls*. *Girls* follows the life of the lead character, Hannah, a role portrayed by Dunham herself. At least somewhat inspired by her own life events, Hannah was a recent Oberlin College graduate who had to navigate life in New York City without the financial support of her parents, which she had become accustomed to. The show was instantly heralded by numerous progressives as a landmark series—a biopic of feminist love literature. Female writers rushed to express their love for the new and *daring* content:

> *But this year, from the fierce and loyal Katniss Everdeen of* The Hunger Games *to the deeply flawed and selfish Mavis Gary in* Young Adult, *I'm finally finding women in film and TV that resonate with me. And no one has got my personal zeitgeist as right as Lena Dunham in her terrific new HBO series,* Girls.[93]

So "right" had Dunham captured the feminist zeitgeist that in its first couple of seasons, *Girls* received numerous awards, including Emmys and Golden Globes. By 2013, Dunham was included in *Time* magazine's list of the most influential people in the world.[94] The success of the show catapulted her to fame, but what exactly was it about the show that elicited such cultural celebration?

It was the fact that Hannah and her friends had fully embraced ugliness.

> *The show's main characters engage in "grotesque" activities such as masturbation, urination or leaving snot in the bathtub. And who can forget Hannah threatening to*

*"pollute" her hostile, dysfunctional, buttoned-up cousin
Rebecca with her "chachie hands", or blithely to "spread"
her underwear-less crotch all over a chair in the apartment she shares with Elijah?* [95]

Lena had produced a series that was intent on destroying all aspects of femininity, instead offering characters that
were unattractive, rude, and, at times, displayed animalistic
attributes. There was no decorum. If Gloria Steinem could
be hailed a heroine for telling women in the '70s to ditch the
housewife bun, Dunham would become a superheroine by
telling them to ditch any and every idea of subjective beauty
and propriety altogether: embrace being fat, embrace being
ugly. And if you desire to overachieve, embrace being both
of those things while naked. Dunham cemented her place
as a challenger to "conventional Hollywood ways, where the
female form must be slim, perfect and hyper-sexualised, or
everyone's eyeballs would spontaneously melt out of their
sockets in sheer disgust."[96] Instead, Dunham was proving that
women could have layers of obese, tattooed flesh and still
demand to be seen. The media rushed to give this unusual
movement a name: body positivity.

Lena became obsessed with the unexpected commercial
success of her ugly brand. Off-screen, she displayed the

personal attributes of the fictionalized Hannah in her real life. Proudly attaching her flag to the mast of "body-positive women," Dunham "fearlessly" took her clothes off at every possible opportunity, even long after the series had finished.[97] And in addition to her routine nudity, fans learned that Dunham also loved to swear.[98] She also loved to talk about her sex life.[99] In general, she became an example of acquiring fame through what has come to be known as *oversharing*. She became addicted to inviting viewers into the most intimate, grotesque parts of her life, and then demanding that they not look away or offer any ill comment lest they be accused of misogyny.

Conservatively, I would estimate that Dunham, who stands at 5 feet, 3 inches, weighs in at about 230 pounds. Factually speaking, she is clinically obese.

Despite this, in January 2020, the actress (looking larger than usual) resolved to share on social media a photo she captured of herself in a bikini. She included a long caption about the importance of accepting the amount of weight she had gained during the COVID-19 lockdown. "I've been thinking a lot about my pot belly in quarantine especially as I notice an unusual amount of articles with titles like 'how I lost weight' and 'diet is everything,'" Lena wrote. "Somehow, headlines that used to roll off my flesh rolls sting in a new way."

To restate this, Lena was communicating to her fans that online content centered around the importance of losing excess weight and eating healthy was harmful to her self-esteem. In fact, she even went so far as to publicly state that "the suggestion of a revamped clean eating plan feels like a personal assault." This thought process has become one of the core tenets of this particular feminist ideology; rather than assuming personal responsibility for a harmful lifestyle and considering how your choices may affect your overall health, the body positivity movement and its advocates' insistence on radical blame followed by acceptance. Radically blame society and accept the worst parts of yourself—ones that you can clearly change.

The comments on Lena's picture were overwhelmingly in praise: "Love everything you say and do and stand for!" "Really important message. Thanks for your courage." "This post is everything. Love you." "I love your honesty. You are beautiful!"

Lena had become used to this kind of public fawning. In fact, a couple of years prior to her COVID-19 weight gain, she shared a before-and-after photo of herself that showed a nearly thirty-pound weight gain. She told her followers that nonstop snacking and eating had made her "happy, joyous, and free," and she ended the post by publicly celebrating her "back fat." The comment section was beyond parody. Suffice it to say that Dunham had become a feminist icon.

Of course, it should register as shocking that what Lena Dunham promotes is objectively harmful to women.

Imagine an alternate universe in which I've created a social media account celebrating anorexia. In this universe, I would routinely post sunken-eyed selfies of myself in lingerie, spiky ribs poking out of my abdomen. I would accompany the photos with long, pointed captions about the many nights I spent contemplating the lack of societal appreciation for my ninety-pound frame and how dehumanizing it is to have doctors and family refer to me as ill. I would simultaneously encourage the young women in my comment section to embrace the bony bodies they were given, dismissing all comments to the contrary as having originated from the patriarchy. Perhaps I might caption the post, "I've been thinking a lot about my bony body during quarantine, especially as I'm seeing more articles than usual about recipes we can make at home. The repeat suggestion to eat feels like a personal assault!" For good measure, I would share a before-and-after photo of myself having shed thirty pounds within a short period of time and assure people that "not snacking or eating has rendered me happy, joyous, and free"!

Would the comment section be littered with praise? Of course not.

The truth is that if the general public came across an Instagram account flagrantly promoting anorexia, it would immediately be reported as harmful content. Mothers everywhere would protest against such pictures and videos, insisting that it was setting a dangerous example for already-struggling teens who were wrestling with body image. In fact, this is *exactly* what happened in 2019 when Instagram was pressured by concerned users, experts, and the media to crack down harder on pro-anorexia content found on their platform.

The Guardian reported that there were thousands of photos and hashtags encouraging and praising anorexia,[100] and that many of them encouraged unhealthy weight goals. Experts went on record to condemn any type of "thinspiration" posting as psychologically damaging. "Instagram has attracted a community focused on anorexia that at times can promote the practice, which could lead to increased health risks including self-harm," Jennifer Grygiel, social media expert and assistant professor of communications at Syracuse University, told *The Guardian*. Other experts echoed her sentiment. The chair of the eating disorders faculty at the Royal College of Psychiatrists, Dasha Nicholls, insisted,

"We have to take down graphic images of eating disorders. There is good evidence those most vulnerable are likely to access those sorts of sites. There is a social obligation and whether there is also an industry obligation is an important point that is coming out at the moment as well."

Following suit, teenagers confessed that the pro-anorexia accounts worsened their eating disorder symptoms and made it nearly impossible to find healing. People pointed to the suicide of British teenager Molly Russell as a harrowing example of what can happen when body image content and self-harm images go unchecked on Instagram. Sadly, fourteen-year-old Molly ended her own life in 2017 after a great deal of content she posted about her struggles went unnoticed.

Our culture doesn't take anorexia lightly, and rightfully so. It is an eating disorder that has destroyed the lives of millions. It ravages the body and mind, paving the way for chronic disease and is often linked to severe mental health issues. Anorexia should not be celebrated, no matter how badly we may feel for the women who suffer from this disease.

Curiously, however, the disease isn't nearly as devastating as obesity, which either receives a pass or routine glorification from the same media and experts. According to the National Association of Anorexia and Associated Disorders, within the United States, there are approximately 10,200 deaths per year from eating disorders, including anorexia, binge-eating, bulimia, and others.[101] Now, weigh that against the approximate 330,000 deaths that are attributed annually to the obesity epidemic in America.[102]

Over 42 percent of Americans were obese in 2017–2018, and the numbers continue to rise as the years go on.[103] The rate of obesity has tripled over the last fifty years, and the CDC estimates that medical care for obese individuals costs the United States $147 billion a year.

The strange, modern feminist insistence on "body positivity" is at least partly to blame. This message is being uniquely sold to women by women. There are now even "body-positive" models. One of the more well-known figures is Tess Holliday, who rose to fame largely for being large. In October 2018, wearing skimpy lingerie, she graced the cover of a *Cosmopolitan UK* issue with the headline "Tess Holliday Wants the Haters to Kiss Her Ass." She was immediately championed as a beacon of hope. Fans poured out support, with many expressing that the magazine cover had changed their life for the better.[104] Celebrities offered their praise and were in awe of her bravery. *Cosmopolitan UK's* editor, Farrah Storr, vehemently defended the magazine's decision to put Tess on the cover, lecturing Piers Morgan on *Good Morning Britain* that the photo would improve the mental well-being of young women everywhere.

"We have a crisis with mental health and people feeling terrible about body image," Farrah insisted. "You know things are not black and white ... We live in a culture which venerates being thin." She then claimed the cover would be well worth it "if there are millions of people who see this and say, 'For one day only I'm going to feel good about myself.'"

There's something curious about this editor's line of logic. Storr raises the concern of the mental health crisis among young women, just like the experts did when Instagram was rightfully pressured into removing pro-anorexia content. However, rather than suggesting we shield young women with mental health issues from images of morbidly obese women as a similar antidote, she instead insists that glamorizing obesity would be the correct course of social treatment. *Cosmopolitan* doubled down in its February 2021 issue by featuring clinically obese women wearing athletic wear on its cover with the paradoxical title, "This Is Healthy!"

The "health at any size" trend had been effectively established, another pillar in the feminist pursuit for endless representation.

On the topic of representation, it's worth noting that it is feminist make-believe that prior to the "body positive" movement, every lead female character in film had to be hyper-sexualized and perfect to find success. That stereotype, for better or worse, ended decades ago. As just one of many cultural examples, a film famed for its portrayal of a highly sought after yet physically imperfect female is *Bridget Jones's Diary*, followed by its sequel three years later. The movie's storyline centers around Bridget's average appearance, which somehow made her more desirable to the two leading men.

Wind the clock back a few hundred years, and the majority of Renaissance art portrayed nude women. The nude female was used as a symbol in a variety of imagery. That imagery could be partially erotic, could be personal to the subject, or could be religious in function. Arguably some of the greatest female nudity was connected with religious imagery around Eve and Adam in the Garden of Eden. The nude could be sacred or, as was the case with Bocelli's groundbreaking *The Birth of Venus* from 1485, painted for simply portraying beauty. If we use the five-hundred-year-old Bocelli's *Venus* as a case in point, we can see that his portrayal of classical female beauty would mirror our concept of what constitutes classical female attraction to this day. *Venus* is not insanely skinny; she has soft curves and childbearing hips. In nearly all the cases of the female nude in art, right up until the twentieth century when the modernist schools take over, the women being painted are what we would describe as normal—neither overweight nor anorexic. In essence, most of the women throughout generations of art have a Body Mass Index within a healthy range. Grossly overweight, however, was never considered to be a classical portrayal of beauty.

What feminists are fighting for then is not to normalize a range of bodies that were evidently already normalized, but rather to normalize a gross extreme.

In 2022, Dr. Jordan Peterson tweeted a picture of plus-sized model Yumi Nu on the cover of the 2022 *Sports Illustrated* Swimsuit Issue with the caption "Sorry. Not beautiful. And no amount of authoritarian tolerance is going to change that."[105] Cue moral outrage. *Forbes* writer Dani Di Placido wrote, seemingly not aware of the inherent contradiction:

> *It goes without saying that physical attractiveness is entirely subjective, and despite Peterson's personal preferences, a lot of people find Yumi Nu to be extremely attractive. If Peterson doesn't, that's ok—frankly, no one asked his opinion on the matter.*[106]

One assumes that Di Placido willfully ignored the fact that nobody asked for his opinion either, but I digress. Peterson earned the ire of not just *Forbes*, but an entire progressive mob. Clinical obesity, as they had determined, would not only be deemed healthy but also beautiful.

It turns out that Dr. Peterson isn't the one refusing this narrative bait. In fact, all it takes is one quick look around the world of media to see that the body positivity trend is exclusively marketed to women. Never have we seen a male actor, singer, or influencer on the covers of *GQ* or *Men's Health* who is morbidly obese, claiming that men can be handsome and sexy at any size. It's difficult to imagine seeing an obese man modeling Calvin Klein underwear on billboards. Simply put, men would never buy into such objective, clinical madness, which is why male digital spaces have remained impervious to the fat acceptance movement.

But what is it about women, specifically, that makes us vulnerable to such nonsense trends?

Throwing it back to basic biology guiding human sociology, women (somewhat ironically) can blame femininity. It's our high emotional IQ which drives us to care for our families and our children, interpret a baby's cry, and nurture those who are in need. But our immense compassion, as we have explored, can be hijacked to our own detriment. In essence, women are empathetic to those that are struggling. That includes a level of empathy for fat woman.

And why shouldn't our hearts ache for women who are overweight and struggling with self-esteem issues? We hate to see young girls wrestle with their awkward adolescence and their insecurities about fitting in. It's painful to witness because each one of us has been through similar experiences at some point in our lives and can empathize. But our ability to empathize can sometimes trump our ability to think logically. We fall prey to the body positivity movement—even though we know it's wrong—because our emotions get the best of us. We can feel so sorry for someone that we become unwilling to speak truth.

Women are therefore lying to Lena Dunham in her comments sections on social media because they feel bad for her. Of course she does not look amazing, and of course, the women telling her that she does know that.

Body positivity is a self-destructive pillar of modern feminism. The feeling of self-acceptance a young woman might feel after seeing a morbidly obese model on the cover of her favorite magazine will be fleeting, but the long-term effects of an unhealthy diet, a sedentary lifestyle, and a refusal to look after her own health can follow her for a lifetime.

And like all categories of modern feminism, although billed as a middle finger to the patriarchy and its unrealistic beauty standards, it is anything but. Ultimately, the body positivity movement is a sad-girl movement. It's what happens when women who were picked last in gym class and were picked last by men gain power and misplace their anger. They are fundamentally angry at women who demonstrate more self-control than they do. They don't think they can obtain objective beauty, and so they seek to destroy the concept of it altogether. The body positivity movement was created by bitter women who feel starved for attention and are willing to take the unconventional route of publicly humiliating themselves to get it.

We've watched Lena Dunham endure some painful moments since she rose to fame. Her six-year relationship with singer and songwriter Jack Antonoff ended in flames, and not long after they split, he was publicly linked to a blonde bombshell, model Carlotta Kohl (a woman who most certainly *did not* prescribe to the body-positive message). Not long after, at only thirty-one years of age, after battling years of painful endometriosis, Lena underwent a hysterectomy in which her uterus, cervix, and one ovary were removed.[107] One of the lifelong side effects of the surgery is that she will never have biological children of her own. She has shared her mental health struggles with anxiety, admitting that it led to an addiction to prescription medicine for which she checked herself into rehab in 2018.[108]

Refusing to deal with her own issues, she instead blames the feminist boogeyman—"the patriarchy"—for setting unrealistic beauty standards and pressuring the world to conform to "normative" family structure. She instead blames the patriarchy for what feminists are now referring to as a "fertility industrial complex" that favors wealthy White women.

Unsurprisingly, Dunham is also a political activist for all the usual causes. She campaigned for Hilary Clinton, professing that she was "pretty worked up about the possibility of a woman President: it's something I thought was impossible, maybe even illegal, when I was a little girl."[109] Quite why she thought this was illegal is utterly confounding, but in a feminist world of pretend problems, why not? Dunham also campaigned for guns to be removed from the movie posters of *Jason Bourne*.[110] She wrote a letter in favor of illegal immigration.[111] She supports the LGBTQ+ agenda. Problems for Lena Dunham are everywhere—except within herself.

In this way, Dunham is not just one woman—she is a class of woman: the late-stage millennial in their thirties or early forties, overweight, affluent, little to non-existent beauty regime, works in a job that should not really exist, studied a soft academic subject at a college that has campus liaisons for equity and inclusion. They are likely signed up to whichever social justice campaign validates their lifestyle. Whether that's the fat acceptance movement, the latest racial justice protest, or the "trans women are women" movement, this particular breed of feminist won't make it to the gym but will always make it to the front of the protest line with a meaningless placard and bullhorn. Because yelling externally allows them to avoid the internal scream of their own unhappiness until they can no longer ignore it. And by then, it's usually too late.

Make no mistake that the Dunham School of Feminism, if not abandoned early enough, will lead to sadness and solitude.

Or worse, death.

6

THE KARDASHIAN SCHOOL OF PLASTIC

There is no question that sexual promiscuity is now mainstream in American culture. Just a few short decades ago, it would have been very rare indeed to see a naked woman flaunt her figure in a public space. It would have been shunned and criticized by mainstream standards. Today, on the other hand, softcore pornography has become the media norm.

Sitting in stark, superficial contrast to the Dunham School of Feminism comes the Kardashian School of Plastic. Of course, the thought leader in this mold is Kim Kardashian. Originally a stylist, Kim Kardashian first appeared across TV screens in 2005. While working with her two sisters, Khloe and Kourtney, at a family clothing boutique called Dash, the idea of a reality TV show was born. *Keeping Up With The Kardashians* went on to become one of the most successful reality television programs ever created in terms of cultural impact and viewing. Kim used the show's success to branch into merchandise, books, films, music, and fashion. In 2014, she married rapper Kanye West, cementing her as an A-list, globally-recognized celebrity. Her name is a marketing juggernaut. She became a billionaire through the development of her SKIMS shapewear and lingerie line. In short, since she first appeared on our screens in 2005, Kim has become, with the exception of perhaps a few global leaders, one of the most recognizable brands on the planet. So, the real question is: How did she do it?

If you look at a picture of Kim now compared to 2005, you would struggle to say you were looking at the same woman. I'm not talking about aging, because I wouldn't say Kim *has* necessarily aged. I'm talking about skin, facial recognition, and body structure. There is an early picture of the three Kardashian sisters, Kim, Khloe, and Kourtney, when they were running the Dash boutique. In the picture, all three of the girls have a hometown attractiveness to them. None of them look like they are going to win Miss Universe, but they have a natural aesthetic.[112] Wind the clock forward to today, and a similar picture of the three sisters shows a hyper-glamorized, artificially perfect, sexualized physique. This is particularly relevant for Kim. She has, with incredible success, sold every physical piece of herself to achieve global celebrity.

Nothing could more aptly demonstrate this soul sale than the infamous Ray J sex tape. Kim and Ray J, the well-known R&B singer, dated from 2002 to 2006 and allegedly filmed themselves getting intimate while on vacation in Mexico. In 2007, the footage became public and was obtained by Vivid Entertainment. At the time, Kim protested the release and alleged that she explored legal action to stop it. It was a compelling topic of conversation in the first season of *Keeping Up With The Kardashians* as she cried over the possibility of additional tapes being released. In essence, the sex tape, which she claimed was leaked without her knowledge, became the controversy that brought her early viewers and media attention.

That's why the world was shocked when, in 2022, her ex-boyfriend and sex-tape partner, Ray J, went public in an interview with the *Daily Mail,* stating that the entire scandal was manufactured by the Kardashians themselves. After fourteen years of staying in the shadows and allowing his reputation to be smeared, Ray J finally came forward with the truth that made a lot more sense than anything before it: Ray J, in coordination with Kim and her famous "momager" Kris

Jenner, organized the filming and release of the sex tape to make Kim famous. In the *Daily Mail* interview, Ray J claimed:

I've never leaked anything. I have never leaked a sex tape in my life. It has never been a leak. It's always been a deal and a partnership between Kris Jenner and Kim and me and we've always been partners since the beginning of this thing.[113]

In that same interview, Ray J admits that the original idea came from him after seeing the success of Paris Hilton's leaked sex tape. Kris and Kim apparently liked his idea and enlisted the help of Vivid Entertainment to execute it. At some point, a contractual agreement was drawn up between Ray J and Kim, with Kris overseeing the sale of the pornography they produced.[114] In private messages shared by Ray J between him and Kim, she did not deny his version of events.[115] Truly incredible.

Of course, despite the decades-long performance as a victim of her own sex tape, it wasn't the last time Kim would appear naked on the internet. In 2010, Kim posed on the front cover of *W* magazine fully nude with the words, "It's all about me, I mean you, I mean me," spread out over her genitalia. Then, in a piece titled "Break the Internet, Kim

Kardashian" for *Paper* magazine, Kim again appeared fully nude. She also appeared partially naked on the July cover of *GQ* while clutching a leather jacket over the front of her body. *Stylecaster* even ran the headline: "Kim Kardashian Returns to Her Preferred State of Being: Naked on a Magazine Cover."[116]

Kim, in conclusion, loves to get naked, giving credence to Ray J's claim that her early protestations were little more than manufactured, reality TV controversy. Somewhat refreshingly, she has made no second attempt at the victim narrative. She is clear in her willingness to sell her body to public eyeballs.

It should be noted that Kim was slow to embrace the feminist title. In fact, she went so far as to actually publish an essay on her website in 2016 titled, "Why I Don't Label Myself a Feminist."[117] That essay, which has since been removed from most publicly available places on the internet, outlined why Kim initially thought of herself as someone who was not a feminist. Her reasoning pertained to "labels" and how they can change perception.[118] But despite her initial protestations, Kim soon realized the inherent benefits of modern feminism. A year later, in an interview with *Harper's Bazaar Arabia*, Kim updated her stance. She claimed:

"I said once before that I'm not really a feminist. But I feel I do a lot more than people that claim that they're

feminist. To clarify what I said before: I feel in my soul I'm a feminist."[119]

To reiterate, Kim experiences feminism on a soul level and recognizes that she does a lot more for women than others who follow its ideology. But what exactly *does* Kim do a lot more of than other women?

Similar to the Dunham School of Feminism, the Kardashian school teaches that nudity is an act of empowerment. Kim Kardashian has defended her decision to pose nude on her own platform, as well as in magazines and photo shoots.

"I am empowered by my body. I am empowered by my sexuality," she wrote in an essay for International Women's Day in 2016 that has since been deleted. "I am empowered by showing the world my flaws and not being afraid of what anyone is going to say about me. And I hope that through this platform I have been given, I can encourage the same empowerment for girls and women all over the world."[120]

Okay ... so Kim Kardashian, who has spent millions on cosmetic procedures to perfect her body and to stop it from undergoing its natural aging process, wants the world to believe that she routinely displays her naked body in an effort to help young girls.

Now let's see how Kim reacted when a teenaged girl respectfully approached Kim about her incessant nudity.

In 2016, actress Chloë Grace Moretz, then just nineteen years of age, came across one of Kim Kardashian's more shocking naked photos on the internet. In the photo, Kim was fully naked, with two thin black bars photoshopped over her breasts and private parts so it wouldn't violate the social media nudity policy. "When you're like I have nothing to wear LOL," Kim wrote in the caption.

Chloë had the guts to reply on Twitter: "I truly hope you realize how important setting goals are for young women, teaching them we have so much more to offer than just our bodies." For Chloë, this photo had a deeper significance for the millions of young women across the globe who idolize Kim. It seemed that Chloë was simply posing the question: Wasn't there a more respectful and dignified way to be confident in your own skin?

Chloë was met with a public onslaught from rabid "feminists" who were suddenly out for blood. Celebrities (including Emily Ratajkowski) and fans accused her of slut shaming and espousing archaic values that set back the women's rights movement. They told Chloë she was merely jealous because her figure would never live up to Kim's. They made fun of her appearance and her age. They lectured her about the freedom women should be granted in their wardrobe choices, whether they choose to don a burka or take off their bra.

Kim, thirty-eight years old at the time, issued a snarky response to Chloë. "Let's all welcome @ChloeGMoretz to twitter, since no one knows who she is. Your Nylon cover is cute boo," she tweeted. Apparently there was no room for conversation on the matter. Chloë was the enemy for daring to challenge the pillars of modern feminism, and the way to deal with her was to mock her for not having achieved enough fame.

Kim's younger sister, Khloe Kardashian, got in on the action—scouring the internet for photos of Chloë and sharing what she believed to be an unflattering photo of Moretz in a bikini, that appeared to be captured by the paparazzi. Her intention was clear: You are ugly and therefore should not comment on my sister.

The assembly of mean girls wasn't quite finished. Days later, Kim met up with supermodel Emily Ratajkowski, a woman who is notoriously praised by the feminist mob for using her nude body to fight the patriarchy. Kim posted a photo on her Instagram of herself and Emily—both topless—with the caption, "When we're like ... we both have nothing to wear LOL."

In short, a group of feminists who routinely get naked to "help young women" ganged up on a teenager by implying that she was too ugly and too unknown to ask them questions about whether their regular displays of nudity was ultimately helping or hurting young women.

As brief of a feud as this may have been, it spoke volumes about the duplicitous state of modern feminism. For many women, it's simply a word that is meant to shield them from further criticism or investigation. What so triggered them about Chloë Grace Moretz's simple question was that it risked exposing the true nature of their public persona.

Simply put, these women are engaging in a modern form of prostitution. They create softcore pornographic material, knowing that such content will increase their online following, which they can sell for profit to advertisers. Kim's original sex tape was hardcore pornography and it arguably launched her career. Other women—just look at OnlyFans as an example—have clearly followed suit. Unwilling to admit that they have resorted to the world's oldest profession, they instead attempt to dignify their act by threading it through a quilt of faux-feminism.

Of course, the Kardashian school is not just one woman anymore. Kim has become, in essence, an entire mold of women. Whether it be Emily Ratajkowski, who quite literally became famous by appearing completely nude in a music video; or Megan Fox, who once boasted about cutting a hole in her jumpsuit so she could have spontaneous sex with her fiancé Machine Gun Kelly,[121] the women in this school are all the same. They are plastic symbols who are willing to spend their lives under the knife to maintain their appearances—hence the never-ending surgical enhancements, makeup routines, and luxurious spending. Somewhat ironically, these women are set upon a quest to keep the one thing they most certainly cannot: their youth.

Prostitution and pornography have never been considered among the trades that benefit women. These women instead set other women upon the same path of degradation, chaining women to rituals of sex and seduction as the only means to garner success. Today, films and television shows are filled with raunchy sex scenes, magazines routinely issue explicit articles about anal sex, countless social media accounts feature nudity, and OnlyFans continues to rise in popularity as young women willingly choose to exploit themselves online for additional income.

It is utterly laughable to suggest that these rituals are done in an effort to defeat the patriarchy. Women offering their naked bodies for free is hardly something that men are going to file a complaint over.

In an essay titled "Men Did Greater Things When It Was Harder to See Boobs," author Amy Otto laments the loss of a society that she marks as "BKK" or "Before Kim Kardashian's breasts were available as an everyday experience." Otto notes that in that previous world, women actually had more power:

Men also used to marry younger and in larger numbers to lock down their very own real-life woman. Now, why bother doing the decent work of marrying and raising a family if you can swipe right and see a new pair every night? "Seventy percent of American males between the ages of 20 and 34 are not married, and many live in a state of 'perpetual adolescence' with ominous consequences for the nation's future," says Janice Shaw Crouse, author of Marriage Matters.

In a bizarre gambit to gain equality, women gave away a ton of the power they had accumulated in society. They held a majority of the cards in sexual relationships and, facing a royal flush, decided to fold. Women used to set the cultural standards and parameters for intimate activity. Now often the guys wield more power over sex and the girls are working way too hard, way too soon, for no reciprocity. More widely available hookups have made men less likely to commit.[122]

Men too are suffering consequences from our increasingly pornographic culture as addiction to sex renders them weaker. According to data from Pornhub, the world's largest internet pornography website, they received 42 billion visits to their website in 2019. Within America, the statistics are as follows: about 200,000 people are classified as "porn addicts," 40 million American people regularly visit porn sites, 35 percent of all internet downloads are related to pornography, 34 percent of internet users have experienced unwanted exposure to pornographic content through ads, pop up ads, misdirected links, or emails, and one third of porn viewers are women.[123]

I would offer that modern feminists, insisting on the need to expose their body parts freely on the internet, offer the gateway drug to such damning societal hobbies and addictions. It should come as no surprise that Lena Dunham has consistently voiced her support for Kim's online presence. "I support experiments in female identity exploration," wrote Dunham in an Instagram caption regarding Kim's book, *Selfish*, a collection of her half-naked selfies over the years.

What the Dunham and Kardashian school have in common is an underlying sadness. It's hard to imagine that a woman with Kardashian's wealth, power, and status could be anything but happy, but a closer examination of her personal life reveals an interesting predicament. Despite being a symbol of sex and monetizing seduction, Kim has failed at relationships. At just forty-four years of age, Kim has already been through three failed marriages. This seems to be the curse of virtually all women who make a career of exposing themselves on the internet. It seems that while most men would jump at the opportunity to sleep with these women, few consider them marriage material, and those that do are perhaps suffering from their own addiction to sex.

Kanye West, Kim's latest husband and father to her four children, admitted that he suffered from such an addiction since childhood. "Some people drown themselves in drugs, and I drown myself in my addiction—sex," he stated in an interview for Apple TV.[124] In that same interview, he blames his addiction for leading to the "breakdown of his family." It is darkly ironic then that Kim routinely produces content that can form and feed addictions to pornography and that ultimately contributed to the demise of her marriage.

In that same spirit, Emily Ratajkowski, who, in 2014, was ranked the third most desirable woman in the world and the fourth sexiest woman in the world, must have been shocked by the breakdown of her marriage to movie producer Sebastian Bear-McClard. Because despite being so undoubtedly hot and desirable, it was widely reported that her husband routinely cheated on her. People everywhere were shocked by the reports—who would cheat on someone so evidently sexually attractive? Responding to the public reaction in a podcast, Emily commented, "It was so interesting that that was the reaction to that news because I was just like 'duh, men are trash ladies.' Like, it doesn't matter who you are or how perfect you are."[125]

Interesting that Emily is correctly able to identify her husband's actions as trash but not her own. What man, outside of one that is struggling internally, would want to be married to a woman who routinely displays her naked body to millions of men worldwide? It is utterly perverse to suggest that in the name of feminism, a man needs to be comfortable sharing his wife's body with the world.

In an interview with *Forbes*, Emily said, "Making a career off of my body and my sexuality and then calling myself a feminist and talking about issues around empowerment has always been kind of controversial."[126] Sadly, it looks to be the case that Emily Ratajkowski lost her husband to the same culture of overt sexuality that she promotes.

I'd be willing to bet that Chloë Grace Moretz will find herself luckier in marriage.

Fortunately, we don't have to imagine where a woman who dedicates her entire life to trying to shock the public with nudity will wind up. Imagine for a moment that you walked into a furniture store with your family. As you're looking around, you notice a sixty-three-year-old woman who is nearly naked. She's wearing a black push-up bra with cleavage from breasts spilling from the top. Below she wears only black fishnet pantyhose—her butt fully exposed through them—as well as black stilettos. Suddenly, to your surprise, the woman crawls beneath a bed in the store, leaving just her exposed bottom legs hanging out, reminiscent of the witch in *The Wizard of Oz* when Dorothy's house lands on her. After a few minutes, she repositions herself on top of the bed and begins biting its baseboard.

Any person who encountered such a scene would immediately alert a store employee, who would in turn call the police. The clinical assumption would be that the woman was suffering from some sort of a psychosis. A more sympathetic determination might be that the woman is ill and perhaps in need of the paramedics. Suffice it say that not a single person would deem this behavior to be remotely appropriate, least of all in a public place.

This is not an entirely fictionalized account. It is precisely what took place on Instagram when pop superstar Madonna, then sixty-three years old, chose to upload photos of herself half-naked, in bondage style lingerie, atop and beneath a bed. The images were so graphic that Instagram took the rare action to remove some of them for violating their nudity policy due to her exposed nipples.

Undeterred, Madonna chose to reupload the images to the social media site, this time with her nipples slightly covered and with the following caption:

> I'm reposting photographs Instagram took down without warning or notification ... The reason they gave my management ... was that a small portion of my nipple was exposed. It is still astounding to me that we live in a culture that allows every inch of a woman's body to be shown except a nipple ... Can't a man's nipple be experienced as erotic?!! And what about a woman's a** which is never censored anywhere. Giving thanks that I have managed to maintain my sanity through four decades of censorship ... sexism ... ageism and misogyny. Perfectly timed with the lies we have been raised to believe about the pilgrims peacefully breaking bread with the Native American Indians when they landed on Plymouth Rock! God bless America."[127]

Setting aside her inexplicable rant against the Thanksgiving holiday and how she manages to, rather confoundingly, relate it to her nipple—there's a lot to unpack here. What Madonna employs is the same tactic that we've seen across the board with this particular new school of modern feminism. The women behave in a way that is publicly unacceptable, and when the public does not accept it, they hide behind words like *ageism* and *sexism* to deem themselves immediately beyond reproach.

But this time, the public wasn't biting. Typically filled with messages of support and encouragement, this time the comment section beneath Madonna's crude photos signified a shift in public sentiment. It seemed a growing number of her fans were suddenly pleading with her to behave more respectfully. "I used to love you back in the 80s and listen to your music when you were normal and actually good," wrote one user. "Nobody wants to get old, me included. You just need to accept it as part of life and just go with it as graciously as possible. But you are in denial and have turned yourself into a freak." Similarly, Curtis Shephard, known by his artist name "50 Cent," publicly mocked the photo. "That's Madonna under the bed trying to do 'Like a Virgin' at 63 [years old]. She shot out if she don't get her old ass up," he wrote. Clearly hurt by his public mocking, Madonna accused him of being "jealous" and lambasted him for what she saw as "trying to humiliate others on social media."[128]

Frankly, Madonna had humiliated herself, which is perhaps the reason that she has since deleted the photos altogether. As a matter of biological reality, humans do not become more attractive as we advance in age. People were objectively repulsed by the photos because they were not in any way flattering. Regarding her unfound claims of sexism, are there many or *any* examples of male artists who are in their sixties, prancing around nearly naked and being told they look beautiful? Of course, there aren't. Because like all self-proclaimed feminists in this particular school of thought, Madonna is not fighting for equality; she is fighting for special treatment. If Elton John or Mick Jagger posted similar images, they would likely, and rightfully so, be considered perverted.

Madonna routinely makes the claim that any negative commentary regarding her physical appearance is an example of ageism. This was the certainly the case when at the 2023 Grammy Music Awards, the sixty-five-year-old pop star appeared with what can only be described as a brand new face. Once again dressed in bondage lingerie, social media exploded with comments pertaining to her shocking surgical modifications. The consensus was that she looked terrifying. *Time* magazine wrote about the public reaction and made an interesting attempt to dismiss it:

There are other people for whom Madonna's Grammy's face is a mark of desperation and in no way standing up to the patriarchy or the forces of ageism. The anime-esque hairstyle, as well the riding crop and lacy teddy she showed off on Instagram but didn't wear on stage, look to them like mutton dressed as lamb, a performative attempt to proclaim one's immaturity, one's sexual viability, one's transgressive bona fides, in a way that seems to play along with what men want women want to be, rather than to stand up to it … Madonna's face is not the face many people would choose. But then again neither is Madonna's life … maybe we will just get over it. Maybe the kind-of-face-you-get-when-you're-puffed-up-from-an-allergy-to-new-medication will become the new black. I wouldn't put it past Madonna to make that happen. If not, at least she got some attention ahead of her tour.[129]

If the best a sympathetic publication can muster in defense of your appearance is to hope that that looking-like-you-had-an-allergic-reaction will become vogue, it may be time to reassess. Critics and fans alike surmised that her new face had been botched perhaps by too much Botox, filler, or a facelift gone horribly wrong. Forced to acknowledge the drastic change in her appearance, weeks later Madonna posted a photo of her face, writing "look how cute I am now that swelling from surgery has gone down."[130] Though we may never know which particular surgery she was recovering from, the results of the procedure were no more shocking than when, in 2019, she appeared with a dramatically enhanced derriere. Yes, at around age sixty-one, Madonna had resolved to get butt implants.

Which makes it curious that in response to the public backlash, Madonna wrote this on her Instagram account:

Once again I am caught in the glare of ageism and misogyny that permeates the world we live in, a world that refuses to celebrate women past the age of 45 and feels the need to punish her if she continues to be strong willed, hard-working and adventurous.

I have never apologized for any of the creative choices I have made nor the way that I look or dress and I'm not going to start. I have been degraded by the media since the beginning of my career but I understand that this is all a test and I am happy to do the trailblazing so that all the women behind me can have an easier time in the years to come.

Of course, the world most certainly does not have an issue with aging artists. Aretha Franklin, Tina Turner, Elton John, Steven Tyler, and Eric Clapton are just a few of the countless artists who performed or continue to perform beyond their youth without critique. Ironically, the person who clearly has a problem with aging is Madonna herself. She is terrified of growing old and goes through drastic, painful measures in the moot hope she can avoid it. The general public is left watching Madonna humiliate herself repeatedly in an attempt to avoid the one thing we know she most certainly cannot: aging.

And like Kim Kardashian and Emily Ratajkowski, Madonna's personal life reads like a cautionary tale. She had had two failed marriages and has since developed a habit of dating men that are, at a minimum, twenty-eight years younger than her.[131] Their youth is intentional. "She likes the idea of a guy being younger than her daughter. It announces her desirability to the world. Some people may see her as a vampire, feeding off of the young, but, in her mind, she is forever youthful and this helps to prove it," a friend of Madonna's commented to the *New York Post*.[132]

I believe and would argue that the public does not view Madonna as a vampire but as a sexual pervert. Whereas in her mind, she is forever youthful; in more rational minds, she is a mentally disturbed senior citizen unable to come to terms with reality. There will be no shortage of twenty-and thirty-year-old men who are willing to date her for access to her wealth and connections. How this in any way works to defy the patriarchy remains to be seen.

Madonna is an illustration of where the quest for perpetual beauty and youth will land any woman. The Kardashian School of Plastic is underscored by a pathological and insatiable need for attention. Feminism for the students of this ideology is but a word used to distract others from accurately identifying their vapid existence. Still wondering how routine displays of nudity help further female empowerment? They simply don't. Far from it, this repackaged narcissism degrades femininity altogether, defining women by physicality. It's the hyper-sexualization of women that, as stated previously, further removes men from commitment. Women suffer the consequences.

This is why false virtue is a core tenet of both the ugly and plastic schools of feminism. For fear that women may begin noticing the flaws and harms of their contributions, these women ally themselves with various social justice movements, which they hope will distract from the great damage they cause.

Here is where I wish to plant a radically different flag. Young women shouldn't believe that taking off their clothes on the internet equates to more freedom. We shouldn't be told that putting on two hundred pounds is objectively "healthy" or an act of bravery. We also shouldn't be cowed into the blind acceptance of whatever social justice mantra graces the monthly cover of a magazine. Instead, to be a real feminist today is to acknowledge that we don't need feminism to make choices for ourselves. My challenge for every woman is to weigh the goals and objectives in her own life. What do *you* want? What do you think actually brings any personal, long-term, fulfilled happiness? I believe that keeping our clothes on makes us infinitely more desirable. I believe that happiness and family are almost synonymous. And though I know we have our work cut out for us to begin correcting things culturally, I fully believe it is as possible as it is inevitable.

7

ALONG CAME HANNAH

Hannah Wright likely never imagined a scenario where she would become the center of attention. Born as the eighth of nine children in a devoutly Mormon family, her childhood in rural Utah likely consisted of chores, hand-me-downs, sibling tiffs—and incidentally, a lot of love.

Her parents owned and operated a local flower shop. They noticed that from an early age, their daughter had a passion and talent for ballet. When Hannah learned of the Julliard School in New York City (the country's most prestigious university for the performing arts), she began dreaming and working toward enrollment.[133] At the age of fourteen, she earned herself a spot in their summer program, and at seventeen, she was formally admitted as a college undergraduate within bustling New York City.

Her parents were overjoyed that she had made her lifelong dream a reality; although, financially, her move to the Big Apple would stretch them. Hannah decided she could contribute by enrolling in beauty pageants to help pay for school expenses. With her long blonde hair, bright blue eyes, and the physique of a ballerina, this proved to be a fruitful endeavor.

It was the summer before her final year at Julliard when fate would change her trajectory. Back home in Utah, she was introduced to a young Daniel Neeleman while at a college basketball game. Hannah was only twenty-one years old, but she knew she had met her husband. The two married just a few months later.

Also a devout Mormon and one of nine children himself, Daniel moved from Utah to New York City to be with his wife as she finished her last year of school. She quickly became pregnant with their first child, Henry. History was made at Julliard when at just one week old, Hannah held Henry in her arms as she crossed the graduation stage to receive her diploma.

Some twelve years and eight children later, Hannah

Neeleman had somehow amassed an astonishing 10 million followers on Instagram. She and Daniel had long since moved back to Utah and had begun documenting their lives farming and raising children. By now well accustomed to the Kardashian culture of sex and minimal clothing across every social media site, the public was mesmerized by the opposing themes surrounding Hannah and couldn't look away from Hannah baking sourdough bread and milking cows every morning. Wearing little to no makeup and cowboy boots, with a litter of children at her helm, she offered a disruption to the usual algorithms of modern feminism. Daniel tended to their hogs. Hannah seemed to always be either milking their cows or in the kitchen preparing a meal with fresh garden herbs. With chickens, roosters, and an always dirty apron, life on their farm seemed both imperfect and altogether idyllic. And with occasional posts of Hannah performing ballet moves in her muddied boots, they chose to appropriately name their homestead "Ballerina Farm." Hannah soon began selling starter kits for her signature sourdough bread. A family business was born.

The world had grown used to well-kept housewives with their faces pulled and stretched in a desperate bid to hang on to their youth. It had similarly grown accustomed to young Hollywood types who, whether through their fashion or lyrics, were bucking tradition. It had almost all but forgotten the generation of women wearing aprons in kitchens with large families. Until along came Hannah.

But the social tastemakers of the day were not about to allow a prancing Hannah Neeleman to usurp their influence. Not without a fight.

A beauty queen, milking cows on a sprawling, 328-acre farm alongside an army of happy-looking children. How can we destroy her?

That was the seemingly declared mission among the class of working women who had shaped their lives according to the promises of modern feminism. Perhaps Hannah's idyllic social media presence made them question their nine-to-five existence. For the writers among them, they knew that uncomfortable subjects were best handled with smears.

For too long, writers have enjoyed a carte blanche to prod into the personal and professional lives of their subjects, while enjoying relative anonymity as it pertains to their own existence. Students are systematically taught that journalists represent a vital "fourth estate"—meant to protect the common man from the corruption of vested interests.

This is, of course, utter nonsense. More often than not, journalists write to affirm their own beliefs and to influence the masses accordingly. If one seeks to understand what motivated a particular piece, the lifestyle of its writer will furnish the answer.

In May 2024, twenty-eight-year old Megan Agnew became the first journalist to be given unprecedented access to the Neeleman family. At the time of her visitation, Agnew was a well-established features writer for *The Sunday Times*. Before we examine the final product of her visitation and the public response to it, let's first consider the author herself.

One year before she made the farming family the subject of her research, Megan Agnew had endeavored to publish something more personal. Titled "What Men Really Think About Modern Dating—By My Exes," a then twenty-seven-year-old Megan set about interviewing some of her previous paramours. And, fortunately, there were more than a few to choose from. Six, to be exact (who were willing to speak under the condition of anonymity), and an unspecified many more who declined to participate. Megan recounts that she "met one on a dating app and the rest around and about (mutual friends, parties, the pub), [their] relationships lasting between one evening and ten months."[134] What becomes immediately apparent is that Megan Agnew's idea of adventure in youth is quite a departure from Hannah Neeleman's.

Megan first introduces readers to Micah. Writing in first

person, she recaps how they "met at a pub in East London on an evening last summer when I asked him for a lighter. We hopped over a park fence and sat under a tree as the sun came up. He is a great laugh and, by his own admission, a bit of a 'showman.'"

Cigarettes *and* park loitering. Who says romance is dead?

Megan then makes it known that when she dated Micah, they always split the bill, which is something she still does. For the uninitiated, women paying for themselves on dates is one of the newer principles of modern feminism because *women are capable and men shouldn't assume their inability and something something something the patriarchy!* You get the picture.

Megan is therefore surprised to learn that her principled tendences did not leave much of an imprint on Micah. She informs readers that "when [he and I] speak today Micah says he sometimes pays [for his dates]. He says this can stem from insecurity about wanting to seem like a grown-up." One gets the sense that Micah is merely dodging feminist bullets by diagnosing his perfectly ordinary male desire to take care of women as a symptom of his own insecurity.

The piece becomes compelling when you consider what sorts of questions Megan must have asked to garner the responses she received.

She writes that "it surprises [her] when [Micah] says he can't remember the last time he cried."

In a similar emotional vein, she presses him on the murder of Sarah Everard, a young woman who was brutally kidnapped, raped, murdered, and burned by a police officer. Megan asserts that "the murder of Sarah Everard changed things for [Micah]. It prompted a long conversation with his sister about how women cross the road out of fear or carry their keys between their fingers in case they need to use them as a weapon. It was a shock to him. How did he feel when that dawned on him?"

In case it's not yet clear, Megan is not reuniting with exes to learn about modern dating. Rather, she is meeting with them out of a sadistic power play. With the ability afforded to her to publish their names and potentially ruin their lives, she is instead giving them the opportunity to effectively castrate themselves before her, so she opts not to. Megan wants her exes to acknowledge their every inherent male flaw, thereby excusing herself from any feelings of unworthiness for not having been chosen by them. The problem with the many men who didn't stay with her are the many men themselves. Not Megan.

She continues this demented form of absolution when she meets up with Eli, another guy she dated for just six months. She informs readers that "as a teenager, Eli says, he definitely got together with girls who were too drunk, in a way he would never do now. And though it was only a kiss, he was probably more pressuring than he is comfortable with."

It's about as close as any writer can get to casually suggesting their ex is a predator. Readers are to understand that it's rather fortuitous she didn't wind up with Eli. And if his infractions as a teenager were not enough, Megan tosses him a loaded question, asking, "Are guys still threatened by driven women?" Eli is wise to respond with exactly what Megan wants to hear, replying, "'I find it attractive but, yes, 100 per cent. Although that is such a taboo to say now, no one would ever say it. I mean, I could see how people could be intimidated by you." One gets the sense that Eli may have a gun to his head.

The driving point here is that the men who ultimately rejected Megan were either emotionally stunted, seemingly predatory, or intimidated by her career.

Megan continues with unintended hilarity by making sweeping conclusions. She acknowledges that her exes represent "a small—and self-centered—research group, and I [therefore] don't want to use it to make sweeping generalisations about a whole gender. Still, a number of things came up again and again—particularly the attempt to transition away from a lad culture they were exposed to in their formative years. These men are trying to learn the right words, learn a new language. Consent is easier to get right than we think … Restaurant bills are split 50-50 but money and how much of it women make is still unsettling. Women have a limitation on when they can have children. Men, mostly, don't … Your teenage years are a hot mess, your twenties are a muddle—and we are still figuring things out."

Let it be said that no one, not even Megan herself, ought to be foolish enough to believe that she reconnected with six former paramours out of a purely scientific interest in male dating. A more reasonable explanation is that at twenty-seven years old, Megan is arriving at the intersection of biology and ideology, unwilling to accept that biology always has the right of way. At her age, the determined feminist who makes it a point to always split the bill is likely watching a lot of her colleagues and former classmates announce engagements and pregnancies. With the decade of her twenties beginning to sunset, perhaps her promiscuity (trumpeted as something of a sacrament of modern feminism) had not actually been worth the bylines. Maybe she met up with her exes to quiet her own anxieties about why none of them had chosen her beyond a fleeting relationship. Maybe she met up with a small hope that one of them might be interested in rekindling the flame.

We can only speculate as to what the men took away from their reunion with Megan Agnew. I'd hazard a guess that any male sitting across from his cigarette-smoking-ex at a pub via an invitation to participate in a "study" featuring five other men she's slept with—only to find himself peppered with leading questions to support a foregone conclusion that men are inherently problematic (but capable of transformation)—likely left that pub like a bat out of hell. And if he had any sense, he spent the evening in deep prayer, hoping he'd satisfied her questions insomuch that he wouldn't become the latest prey of a feminist hit piece.

That aside, there was something vaguely familiar about the nature of her article—an almost plagiarized aesthetic of a young female writer who was cool and confident enough to publicize the intimate details of her failed relations with men. Indeed, it was an aesthetic molded by a fictional character who came to define an entire generation of young women: Carrie Bradshaw.

It can be argued that single women sharing the private details of their dating lives was made culturally sexy by HBO's hit series *Sex and the City*. Premiering in 1998, the series followed the life of thirty-year-old Carrie Bradshaw (played by actress Sarah Jessica Parker), a sex columnist living in New York City. Carrie was a glamorous socialite with a knack for high fashion. She excelled at transforming the many failed relationships and sexcapades of her and her close girlfriends into philosophical slop for the masses. Each episode concluded with Carrie delivering some impassioned feminist morals, for if feminism had become faith, Carrie Bradshaw had written its gospels. Some sample proverbs are as follows:

"Maybe the best any of us can do is not to quit, play the hand we've been given, and accessorize the outfit we got." [135]

"Being single used to mean that nobody wanted you. Now it means you're pretty sexy and you're taking your time deciding how you want your life to be and who you want to spend it with." [136]

After he left, I cried for a week. And then I realized I do have faith. Faith in myself. Faith that I would one day meet someone who would be sure that I was the one." [137]

"Maybe some women aren't meant to be tamed. Maybe they need to run free until they find someone just as wild to run with." [138]

"The fact is, sometimes it's really hard to walk in a single woman's shoes. That's why we need really special ones now and then to make the walk a little more fun." [139]

"Some people are settling down, some people are settling, and some people refuse to settle for anything less than butterflies."[140]

In short, millennials learned that there was virtually nothing a pair of Manolo Blahnik heels and a Cosmopolitan cocktail shared among girlfriends couldn't fix. Not settling for *anything less than butterflies* became the subconscious motto. With such an impossible standard set, it should come as no surprise that despite six seasons of dating, and an additional two feature-length films, Carrie Bradshaw never had any children. In fact, it was almost as though Carrie had never even considered it. Given the international acclaim of the series, this was not a culturally insignificant omission. Because however fictional, an entire generation of young women began romanticizing the perceived, eternal freedom of Carrie's lifestyle.

What makes it interesting to consider is that her character wasn't entirely born of fiction. In fact, Carrie Bradshaw was inspired by the real-life of the show creator and author, Candace Bushnell. Like the character she would come to create, Bushnell was a freelance writer and socialite living in New York City who penned a newspaper column illustrating the various dating experiences of her and her girlfriends. It was this real-life column that spawned her eventual bestselling book that became the basis for the cult television series. Four years after the series took off, at the age of forty-four, Bushnell married Charles Askegard, a ballet dancer she met at a social benefit. And naturally, her show's protagonist followed suit. In the 2008 blockbuster film *Sex and the City*, Carrie Bradshaw (now in her early forties) makes the decision to marry her longtime boyfriend, "Mr. Big." For extra girlboss posterity, the decision is one of financial practicality rather than traditionalism. Because when Carrie and Mr. Big decide to purchase a luxury condo together, they suddenly wonder, *What will happen if we split up? Easier to just get married!* Once again, the cultural message is significant: A woman can have it all—the career, the friendships, the lifestyle, and eventually (and only if it makes economic sense, of course) the man as well. It was the perfect feature-film ending to a storyline that had lasted twenty years. Viewers rejoiced and demanded a sequel.

Obliging audiences worldwide, *Sex and the City 2* was released in 2010. If there were any questions as to whether the now-lawfully-wedded Carrie could still strike a meaningful feminist chord with audiences, the plotline immediately put that question to bed. Now a couple of years into marriage and still without any children, Carrie is missing the excitement of her single years. She laments the fact that her husband would prefer to stay home and watch movies with her rather than paint the town. The solution? Carrie decides to move into her old apartment for a couple of nights a week so they can each still enjoy the excitement of having individual lives while they are married. And by golly, it works! They discover they are much more attentive to each other when they commit to only a few days a week of cohabitation. And if that isn't modern or feminist enough, elsewhere in the plot, Carrie and her signature girlfriends pack up the Cosmopolitans and head to Abu Dhabi for some much-needed girl time. While there, Carrie runs into one of her exes, a guy named Aidan. When swept up in a moment of reminiscing, the two kiss *(oops!)*. Feeling extremely guilty, she calls her husband back home and informs him of her betrayal. But was it *really* a betrayal? Sure, in your grandmother's outdated, old-fashioned, sacramental concept of a marriage, it might count as one, but this is the happier feminist future. In this modern dream world, women can do no wrong (even when they've clearly done wrong).

Suffice it to say that when Carrie returns home to her part-time marital abode with Mr. Big, she is greeted with a gift by her still adoring husband. He presents her with an expensive black diamond, to be precise. Because as any husband-married to-a-feminist ought to know, if your wife cheats, it's likely because you gave her, well, less than butterflies. And as every woman knows, black diamonds equal butterflies. With their marriage now firmly back on track thanks to a little space and infidelity, the movie concludes with Carrie proverbially informing viewers that she and her husband "found less and less need to escape to the other apartment. But we kept the option open, just in case someone needed those two days off. As for me, I began to think of marriage much like the Real Housewife of Abu Dhabi's veil. You have to take the tradition and decorate it your way."[141]

Yes, in the designer world of Carrie Bradshaw, the conclusion is always this breathtaking. But one does wonder if the application of such daring feminist solutions can work off the big screen.

Interestingly enough, six years into her real-life marriage and just before the release of the sequel film, Candace Bushnell sat down for a long form interview with the *Huffington Post*. When asked whether or not women really could have it all, she responded:

Is it possible to be married, have children, and have a high-powered career? Absolutely. And women do it all the time. And they just get on with it. The key to life is your attitude. But happiness comes out of being willing to do your work in your twenties to find out who you are, what you love. There are lots of studies out there about women who leave their work and it turns out that they didn't like their jobs. We need to encourage young women to find what they love to do. That is a very valuable pursuit — more so than the pursuit of a boyfriend. When you have that core, you bring that core to every aspect of your life ... And I think it's very, very important for women to have their own income. The reality about being economically dependent on someone else usually doesn't work out for women in the end. It's about being an adult and being responsible for your life. Most women have to work, so let's just get on with it ... A hundred years ago, a woman couldn't even have a passport, because she only had an identity in terms of her husband. Of course there were single women, but they were spinsters. Or a woman who stayed home and took care of her parents. It was very difficult for a woman to live her living without being married. And now, because women can earn a living, they can survive being single. Everything is about economics.[142]

Though we can only speculate as to how these perspectives may or may not have informed her marriage, what we do know for certain is that just three years later, Candace

Bushnell filed for divorce, citing her husband's infidelity. Adding further insult to injury, Bushnell alleged that Askegard engaged in an affair with a fellow ballerina who was half her age.[143] To the many women who had invested in her real-life fairytale, this was a tragedy. Because what more could her husband have wanted? He had married a woman who was fabulously rich, successful in her own rite, and in hot demand on red carpets across the world.

We should be clear here that there is never any excuse for marital infidelity. Marriage is a sacred union, and to betray that covenant amounts to sin. But of course, that's only if one holds "traditional" views on marriage. In the modern world dictated by cultural tastemakers like Bushnell herself, her husband may have been merely chasing butterflies. This is said not to mock her pain or to transfer the guilt of his indiscretion but rather to wonder how and if Bushnell is able to reconcile her life's work with its cultural effects.

During her marriage, Bushnell chose not to have children. In 2019, at the age of sixty and with a net worth of over 20 million dollars, she reflected on that decision. Speaking with *The Sunday Times*, the former sex columnist confessed that "when I was in my thirties and forties, I didn't think about it. Then when I got divorced and I was in my fifties, I started to see the impact of not having children and of truly being alone. I don't want to be shot down, but now I do see that people with children have an anchor in a way that people who have no kids don't."[144]

It has been said that wisdom comes with age. Certainly, this later sentiment would have clashed with the overriding narrative of Carrie Bradshaw; a life seemingly fulfilled by booze, promiscuity, and a persistent focus on self. And what of her previously expressed position that women ought to concern themselves primarily with financial security because "everything is about economics"? It seems lessons from divorce and aging had clarified her perspective once again. She told the reporter that, at sixty, "you want someone to be nice; you don't want someone who's critical or demeaning. It feels like when one is younger there can be this competition between partners. Maybe that's part of the sexual attraction, but that kind of stuff just doesn't work when you get older."

Perhaps most shockingly, despite the many Emmy and Golden Globes accrued for creating a series about women aspiring to have sex as often as men, Bushnell confesses elsewhere in the interview that following her divorce, she chose to remain celibate for five years. What a pity that the truer lessons from her life will never earn as much attention as the fictional ones.

There's an episode of *Sex and the City* when Carrie visits

her then-boyfriend's home in upstate New York. She trades her trademark stilettos for muddy boots and overalls, and rather predictably, hates every moment of it. For her, a rustic cabin paired with poor cell phone reception amounts to a medieval torture chamber.

This is how one might imagine Megan Agnew felt arriving from London to middle-of-nowhere Utah to interview Daniel and Hannah Neeleman.

Suffice it to say it was a fait accompli.

Pitched as a "day-in-the-life" profile behind their successful family brand, Daniel and Hannah did not think to research Megan Agnew before agreeing to the piece. Their guard was completely down as they welcomed her into their home, introduced her to their children, and answered her every question about how they manage it all.

Hannah would later reflect that she and Daniel felt the interview went really well, which only added to their shock when Megan published her final piece, titled "Meet the Queen of Trad Wives (and Her Eight Children)."[145] Writing of her experience interviewing the couple, Megan complained, "I can't, it seems, get an answer out of [Hannah] without her being corrected, interrupted or answered for by either her husband or a child. Usually, I am doing battle with steely Hollywood publicists; today I am up against an army of toddlers who all want their mum and a husband who thinks he knows better."

It is remarkable that Megan, who herself requested to interview the family of ten, expresses frustration when she comes into contact with, well, a family of ten. She seems altogether offended by the presence of toddlers. What she describes as disruptive, a happier person might define as joy.

Unaware of her inherent misery, she continues trying to extract pain from normalcy, this time, invoking elements of anxiety and fear:

> I want to ask [Hannah] about birth control, but we are surrounded by so many of her children and Daniel is back in the room now too. Do you—I pause and look at her fixedly—plan pregnancies? "No," Daniel says. "When he says no," Neeleman responds gently, "it's very much a matter of prayer for me. I'm, like, 'God, is it time to bring another one to the Earth?' And I've never been told no."

Sticking with her carefully woven theme of the trapped housewife, Megan informs her readers that the villainous husband Daniel "wanted to live in the great western wilds, so [he and Hannah] did; he wanted to farm, so they do;

he likes date nights once a week, so they go (they have a babysitter on those evenings); he didn't want nannies in the house, so there aren't any." The only space earmarked to be Neeleman's own—a small barn she wanted to convert into a ballet studio—ended up becoming the kids' schoolroom.

The message here is hardly subliminal; Hannah Neeleman is a victim of marital abuse. Readers should know that despite wholesome appearances, Hannah gave up her lifelong dream of dancing to play handmaiden to a controlling man. Sure, that man also happens to be her husband, and they do appear quite happy on Instagram, but after just one day on the farm, the astute Megan Agnew had uncovered a much harder, colder truth: Poor Hannah Neeleman is not even provided an opportunity to express her own desires within her home. And were it not for her cumbersome marriage, she might still be living in New York City, happily dancing ballet.

As if these findings could not get any worse, Megan alerts readers to even more abuses:

They have a cleaner but no childcare; Neeleman does all the food shopping—kids in tow—and cooks from scratch (they "don't do" ready meals). Despite the more traditional aspects of their relationship, Daniel is a hands-on father, taking the kids out to the farm and

doing all the laundry ... Still, Daniel says, Neeleman
sometimes gets so ill from exhaustion that she can't get
out of bed for a week.

You read that correctly. Hannah doesn't buy ready-made meals from the grocery store. And because it likely pained Megan to acknowledge that the villainous Daniel does all the laundry and is active in the child-rearing, she climatically reveals to readers that despite these devotions, Hannah sometimes falls ill from exhaustion. Remarkably, this big reveal is delivered without any further context provided. *Was this said in jest, or in response to a loaded question? And what specifically was even said? Would it not be more prudent to provide readers with an exact quotation when announcing an alleged illness?* With no transcript of the conversation made available, readers are to imagine that Daniel told Megan something along the lines of "Due to the exhausting demands I place on Hannah daily, she sometimes slips into a week-long coma!"

The intentional removal of context and precise quotations to arrive at a foregone conclusion are just a few of many tricks used by journalists who view themselves as guardians of cultural ab-norms. When her hit piece was published, the public backlash to it was swift and immense.

Readers were horrified at the insidious attempt to portray the Neeleman family as dysfunctional and antiquated for having resisted the ill-begotten trends of progressiveness. It seemed that after decades of indoctrination, the public had finally had enough.

The spell had finally broken.

Women flooded social media with angry comments directed at *The Sunday Times*. And though naturally applauded by her coven of colleagues, Megan Agnew was similarly inundated with sharp criticism over the less-than-covert aim of her piece. One week later, in an attempt to dignify her reporting, Megan published a supplementary piece titled "My Day with the Tradwife Queen and What It Taught Me."[146] Further justifying her conclusions regarding the "Mormon homemaker and influencer," Megan reflected:

> *When I asked, Neeleman seemed detached from the politicisation that surrounds her. This was her life, she told me, and she posted about it online. It was that simple. Daniel had more opinions, leading the way when I asked about their stance on abortion, marriage, feminism and the label "trad wives." But the most surprising part of the day—perhaps naively on my part—was trying to talk to her alone. There were so many*

things I wanted to ask which were inappropriate to do so in front of her husband or young children—about contraception, married life, the trials of motherhood, or just simply who she was and what she thought when she was away from it all.

No, Meg. The most surprising part of the day was your belief that there are secrets a woman should be keeping from her husband. And more absurdly, that those secrets ought to be immediately confided to a complete stranger who flew in from London. The most surprising part is that despite your education, you fail to perceive that there can be joy derived from selflessness. What you believed was "Daniel interrupting" is known to those who are happily married as "finishing one another's sentences." To those who cherish the sacrament of marriage, what you observed was a functional family. It's the simple equation of two becoming one and creating many more. It's only upon the spiritually famished tongues of modern feminists that the inherent blessing of family is routinely interpreted as a curse. If Neeleman seemed "detached from the politicization of her brand," it is likely because the natural, biological aim of family should not be reduced to a marketing term.

Of course, most surprised by Agnew's words was Hannah

herself. Taking to her social media profiles, Hannah disputed the published narrative and further clarified her life choices:

A couple of weeks ago we had a reporter come into our home to learn more about our family and business. We thought the interview went really well—very similar to the dozens of interviews we had done in recent memory. We were taken aback, however, when we saw the printed article which shocked us and shocked the world by being an attack on our family and my marriage, portraying me as oppressed with my husband being the culprit. This couldn't be further from the truth. Nothing we said in the interview implied this conclusion, which leads me to believe the angle taken was predetermined. For Daniel and I, our priority in life is God and family. Everything else comes second. The greatest day of my life was when were married 13 years ago. Together we have built a business from scratch, we've brought eight children into this world and have prioritized our marriage all along the way. We are co-parents, co-CEOs, co-diaper changers, kitchen-cleaners and decision makers. We are one, and I love him more today than I did 13 years ago. We have many dreams still to accomplish. We are not done yet having babies, we are excited for our new farm store to open and I can't wait to see what the future holds for the rest of it. But for now, I'm doing what I love most: being a mother, wife, a businesswoman, a farmer, a lover of Jesus. And making meals from scratch.[147]

For the first time since the advent of feminism, tradition beat out modernity. There was something about Hannah Neeleman that had proven a bridge too far for even the tastemakers to cross. The public saw Agnew's piece for what it was: a botched attempt to justify her own life choices. Just as it was with her past paramours, so it went with the Neeleman family. Megan Agnew persecutes what she does not hold in her own life. It is a diabolical form of coveting.

But the diabolical is exactly what the media lauds, which is why the controversy gave Megan Agnew's career an immediate boost. *The Sunday Times* promoted her to the position of senior features writer, and soon thereafter Megan took home the Feature Writer of the Year award at the annual Press Awards.

It is quite stunning to consider that although Hannah Neeleman spoke out to declare that she and her family had been misled, misrepresented, and hurt, the media still found cause for celebration. Presenting accolades to a journalist for successfully deceiving a family is dastardly and cruel.

We can suppose that through the eyes of a modern feminist, Megan felt she had won. After all, she got to take home a glass trophy from the Press Awards. Presumably, it now sits in her quiet apartment, undisturbed by the sound of children who adore her or a husband suggesting where she might place it.

And she can rest assured that she did it for the advancement of women. Because while Hannah exhausts herself working for her family, Megan exhausts herself working for *The Sunday Times*. The publication certainly benefited from the many internet clicks Megan had earned them, which no doubt translated into advertising sales for their newspaper—a newspaper that is one of many sitting beneath the ownership of Rupert Murdoch's publishing dynasty, now formally headed by his son, Lachlan Murdoch.

Take that, patriarchy.

Today, Megan Agnew is thirty years old. As of this writing, she has relocated from London to Manhattan, where she can perhaps more fully embody the Carrie Bradshaw stereotype. Hannah Neeleman is now thirty-four years old and still very much surrounded by the noise of her family on their farm.

Only time (or an iota of common sense) will tell who truly won.

8

HOCUS POCUS

On October 8, 2003, the Broadway play *Wicked* premiered at the Gershwin Theatre in New York City. The story was a reimagination of the witches from *The Wizard of the Oz* in which Elphaba (the traditional wicked witch) is no longer the assumed villain. Instead, she and Glinda (the traditional good witch) are recast as friends who share many hopes and dreams with each other. In one review of the musical that appeared in the online publication, *Junkee*, freelance writer Scarlett Harris writes:

> Wicked *offers an alternative to the marriage and babies and home-owning (oh my!) that are so often part and*

parcel of 'having it all.' The witches break convention with many other Broadway musicals, choosing political activism over love.[148]

The play didn't represent the first time witches had been reimagined in popular culture, particularly across "female-led" television productions. *Sabrina the Teenage Witch* and *Charmed* were successful series that reintroduced the idea of witchcraft as a force for good rather than evil. This transfiguration has also been documented in commentary from national media. In an article titled, "'We Are the Weirdos': How Witches Went from Evil Outcasts to Feminist Heroes,"[149] NPR writer Hazel Cills states:

I think a lot of feminists, like myself, have romanticized witchcraft for a few reasons ... One, it's a woman using powers to change a world that doesn't like her in the first place. A witch tale is a feminist fantasy because it's about having a physical, mystical power that can create real, dangerous change in a world that would rather take power away from them.

Romanticizing witchcraft? This strange concept of inverting heroines was in fact predicted by C.S. Lewis in his novel,

Perelandra. The story takes place on the planet Venus where protagonist Elwin Ransom battles against a satanic character named Professor Weston for influence over the queen. It can be best understood as a dramatic retelling of the story of Adam and Eve. The Queen of Venus represents Eve, and Professor Weston represents the serpent who tries to convince her to violate divine command by going where she is forbidden. Ransom realizes that Weston is attempting to brainwash the queen into committing this violation by telling her stories about heroines who had broken traditional norms:

> *At last it dawned upon [Ransom] what all these stories were about. Each one of these women had stood forth alone and braved a terrible risk for her child, her lover, or her people. Each had been misunderstood, reviled, and persecuted: but each also magnificently vindicated by the event … Ransom had more than a suspicion that many of these noble pioneers had been what in ordinary terrestrial speech we call witches or perverts. But that was all in the background. What emerged from the stories was rather an image than an idea—the picture of the tall, slender form, unbowed though the world's weight rested upon its shoulders, stepping forth fearless and friendless into the dark to do for others what those*

others forbade it to do yet needed to have done. And all the time, as a sort of background to these goddess shapes, the speaker was building up a picture of the other sex. No word was directly spoken on the subject: but one felt them there as a huge, dim multitude of creatures pitifully childish and complacently arrogant; timid, meticulous, unoriginating; sluggish and ox-like, rooted to the earth almost in their indolence, prepared to try nothing, to risk nothing, to make no exertion, and capable of being raised into full life only by the un-thanked and rebellious virtue of their females.[150]

Published in 1943, these words read like a prophecy of modern feminism: women (brainwashed by the idea of some ultimate freedom) convinced they must rise above the persecution of the ordinary by routinely and senselessly rebelling against anything they deem too normative. In the process, these women paint a picture of men as altogether unnecessary. And, of course, any woman who doesn't live up to or wish to participate in this antihero narrative is viewed as "pitifully childish" and "prepared to try nothing." Recognizing the political equality we have with men is forbidden. It's now the case that *any* woman who isn't actively helping to overthrow the mythical patriarchy is viewed as problematic.

What has struck me particularly about the idea of feminism within the context of witchcraft is the evidence that the movement has succeeded at casting spells within society. When it comes to politics, feminists have convinced the public not to believe their own eyes and ears.

And certainly never to believe their own brains.

We've already seen that within the context of the alleged gender pay gap. Despite plentiful evidence that it merely reflects different interests between the sexes rather than discrimination, the myth persists. And there are many more spells the women's movement has cast upon society, seemingly deluding the masses into seeing discrimination where there clearly is none.

A feminist favorite is the false narrative that women's bodies are being controlled in the United States because they are unable to access abortions. The truth, however, is that abortion laws (particularly in states like California and New York) are some of the most liberal in the Western world. The overturning of *Roe v. Wade*, despite feminist shrieks to the contrary, was merely a debate regarding whether the federal government had previously trampled on state's rights by federalizing abortion despite the procedure not being enshrined in the Constitution. In the United States, the federal government can only supersede state laws regarding rights enshrined in the Constitution. So the obvious answer is that yes, the earlier *Roe v. Wade* decision did trample over state's rights and should have been reversed. Since the Supreme Court strictly deals with interpreting the constitutionality of laws, they rightfully determined, in a majority opinion, that abortion was not a constitutional right and therefore was a matter to be decided upon by individual states. In the majority opinion authored by Justice Kavanaugh for *Dobbs v. Jackson*, the Court stated:

> *The issue before this Court, however, is not the policy or morality of abortion. The issue before this Court is what the Constitution says about abortion. The Constitution does not take sides on the issue of abortion. The text of the Constitution does not refer to or encompass abortion ... On the question of abortion, the Constitution is therefore neither pro-life nor pro-choice. The Constitution is neutral ... To be clear, then, the Court's decision today does not out-law abortion throughout the United States. On the contrary, the Court's decision properly leaves the question of abortion for the people and their elected representatives in the democratic process. Through that democratic process, the people and their representatives may decide to allow or limit abortion. As Justice Scalia stated, the*

"States may, if they wish, permit abortion on demand, but the Constitution does not require them to do so."[151]

Hardly the great calamity of outlawing abortion, as feminists proclaimed. Yet the insistence that somehow this represented a patriarchal victory still resounds in leftist echo chambers. And that perhaps is how the spell is cast—through the unrelenting repetition of the word *patriarchy* throughout pop culture, even if it is not accompanied with a shred of proof to support it.

In the 2021 release of Taylor Swift's rerecorded second album, *Red*, Swift chose to amend and extend her old song "All Too Well." The lyrics of one verse infamously included a line that acclaimed "F*ck the patriarchy". Shortly thereafter, she released her tenth studio album, *Midnights*. The debut single from the album is titled "Anti-Hero", which was another strong nod to Swift's growing feminist persona.

Of course, Swift's foray into feminist ideology had long since been documented, as well as who exactly helped to shape her perspectives. In a 2014 interview with the *Guardian*, Swift declared:

I think a lot of girls have had a feminist awakening because they understand what the word means ...

Becoming friends with Lena [Dunham]—without her preaching to me, but just seeing why she believes what she believes, why she says what she says, why she stands for what she stands for—has made me realize that I've been taking a feminist stance without actually saying so.[152]

Swift's impact on modern feminist ideology has been nothing short of impressive. I would describe her as the Goldman Sachs of the feminist movement. Let's start with her music. Most people are surprised to learn that Taylor Swift is (at the time of writing) thirty-five years old. She has brilliantly and successful marketed herself as an angsty teenager who routinely has her heart broken by guys who are undeserving of her affection. More simply put, she has marketed herself as someone who is regularly abused by men emotionally. Her songs drop clues as to whom the always-famous men are, resulting in her millions of mostly adolescent fans working to decipher her lyrics like riddles.

And there have been a lot of men to decipher: fellow musical artists Joe Jonas, John Mayer, Harry Styles, Calvin Harris, and Matty Healy. Actors Lucas Till, Taylor Lautner, Jake Gyllenhaal, Tom Hiddleston, and Joe Alwyn, plus political royalty Conor Kennedy and her current fiancé, football tight end Travis Kelce.

Of course, the purpose of a thirty-five-year-old Taylor Swift playing the part of a teenager is that it grants her access to an army of prepubescent fans prepared to defend her with a sort of rabid, emotional vigor that is unique to adolescents and feminists. In short, any man who harms Taylor Swift will be made to suffer—no further questions asked.

When it comes to Taylor Swift, the fact is that she is not a woman that gets mad in relationships; she gets even.

She told her fans that Joe Jonas notoriously broke up with her in a twenty-seven second phone call back in 2008. The public of course, never got to hear Jonas's version of events, but they hated him anyway.

In 2010, she released a song, widely understood to be about John Mayer, titled "Dear John," in which she accused him of taking advantage of her. Asking a range of leading rhetorical questions throughout the lyrics, she muses whether nineteen is "too young" to have been subjected to his "games". She states that "the girl in the dress" was the one who ended up messed up and crying. She states she loved him. The list goes on. Of course, her fans ate up her vulnerability, casting John Mayer as another villain who had used and abused their princess.

Curiously, however, two years after the release of the song, John Mayer did what most of her exes wouldn't dare—he fired back at her victim narrative. Speaking with *Rolling Stone*, he flat out denied her version of events. "I didn't deserve it. I'm pretty good at taking accountability now, and I never did anything to deserve [what she wrote]," he said. "It was a really lousy thing for her to do." Elsewhere in the interview, he referred to that strategy of music as "cheap songwriting" and an "[abuse] of talent."[153]

It was the first time a man had the audacity to fire back at what was fast becoming a very clearly established business strategy. It certainly wouldn't be the last time.

After Swift dated DJ Calvin Harris for one year, the two decided to call it quits. At the time, Harris had a hit song with pop star Rihanna titled "This Is What You Came For." Unbeknownst to the public, at some point, while they were dating, Taylor contributed some vocals to the track and did not wish to be credited with it. But when they broke up, it seems that she changed her mind. At almost the same time their split was announced, someone conveniently leaked to the press that Taylor Swift had contributed vocals and never received proper credit. It looked like an intentional PR effort to transfer the global success of the track from Calvin to Taylor.

Taylor's fans, of course, read the circumstance as another man using and abusing their talented queen. For Calvin, it was obvious who had leaked the information to the press. He took to Twitter to condemn this attempt, writing, "Hurtful to me at this point that [Taylor] and her team would go so far out of their way to try and make ME look bad at this stage. I know you're off tour and you need someone new to try and bury like Katy [Perry] etc but I'm not that guy, sorry. Won't allow it. Please focus on the positive aspects of YOUR life because you've earned a great one."

It was, without question, the closest that any man had come to calling out Taylor's pattern of abuse. She enters relationship after relationship, and then, on the way out, she attempts to utilize an ill-informed army of teens to settle the score.

To me, this is public witchcraft via the perversion of truth—the person who has routinely and publicly humiliated men (with a legion of tweens prepared to harass them) has managed to convince the public that she is always the victim. Perhaps Katy Perry was correct when, back in 2014, she publicly referred to Taylor Swift as "Regina George in sheep's clothing."

But in 2019, when confronted with what most would describe as a normal business development, Taylor shed her sheep costume and went full wolf.

Before unpacking this incredible event, it's important to first note that Taylor Swift does not represent a rags-to-riches

Hollywood story. In fact, if Taylor had never become famous, she would have had to settle with just being wealthy. Taylor Swift grew up on an idyllic Christmas tree farm in West Reading, Pennsylvania. Her father, Scott Swift, was a stockbroker for Merrill Lynch, and her mother was a marketing executive for a financial fund. They hired a talent manager for their daughter when she was twelve years old, and Scott relocated to Merrill Lynch's Nashville office so Taylor could pursue her career in music two years later.

Suffice it to say that when record executive Scott Borchetta approached her family to sign their daughter in 2005, Taylor was well represented. So well represented, in fact, that her financially savvy father took a 5 percent stake in Borchetta's new company, Big Machine Records. Naturally, there would have been a fleet of lawyers involved from both sides to close the deal. Of course, neither Scott Swift nor Scott Borchetta could have ever predicted Taylor's future success when they orchestrated the deal. They simply agreed to what they both thought was fair at the time.

Borchetta took a chance on an unknown Taylor Swift, and that risk paid off—until Taylor decided it somehow wasn't fair fourteen years later. Taylor decided that she would relitigate her business deal through the tactic which had always served her: manipulating the emotions of her fans who she could assume knew nothing about business.

At the heart of the matter was a man named Scooter Braun who had recently purchased Big Machine Records through his holding company. Through this perfectly legal and normal business transaction, he had acquired the "masters" to the music catalogue Taylor Swift had created while under the label.

For definition's sake, a *master* is effectively an original recording. Whoever owns the master recording controls the destiny of the song. Should any person or company wish to use that song in a TV ad, they must pay a fee to the owner of the master. In this case, Taylor Swift's catalogue was now owned by Braun. But Swift, (who had recently left Big Machine for Universal Music) didn't like that fact. She didn't like Scooter Braun personally either, because she associated him with his client Kanye West and his then-wife Kim Kardashian—who had previously humiliated her by showing the public just how cunning and deceptive Taylor Swift could be.

Kanye had released his song titled "Famous" back in 2016. That song included the now infamous line, "I feel like me and Taylor might still have sex. Why? I made that b*tch famous." Taylor's fans revolted against the perceived misogyny of the line, and Swift had her public relations team issue a public statement distancing herself from the lyrics, driving her fans to direct even more vitriol to the rapper. That was until Kim Kardashian released a recording of Taylor Swift excitedly discussing the song with Kanye, who had run part of the lyric by her to get her approval. On the phone call, he rapped the line to her, but did not use the word "*b*tch*." Taylor, of course, failed to mention that phone call, which would have significantly reduced the hatred Kanye was receiving from her fan base. Instead, she had her public relations team make it look as though she was completely shocked by the lyrics altogether, because … feminism.

Once again, Taylor Swift had been caught convincing the public that she was the victim, when, in fact, she was acting as an aggressor. She therefore wanted nothing to do with Scooter Braun. In her mind, he had orchestrated this public "attack" against her innocent image. So she took to social media to seek her revenge, plus renegotiate the perfectly legal business acquisition of her music.

In a Tumblr post, Swift wrote the following (this is the abridged version):

> For years I asked, pleaded for a chance to own my work. Instead, I was given an opportunity to sign back up to Big Machine Records and 'earn' one album back at a

time, one for every new one I turned in … I had to make the excruciating choice to leave behind my past. Music I wrote on my bedroom floor and videos I dreamed up and paid for from the money I earned playing in bars, then clubs, then arenas, then stadiums.

Some fun facts about today's news: I learned about Scooter Braun's purchase of my masters as it was announced to the world. All I could think about was the incessant, manipulative bullying I've received at his hands for years. Like when Kim Kardashian orchestrated an illegally recorded snippet of a phone call to be leaked and then Scooter got his two clients together to bully me online about it… Or when his client, Kanye West, organized a revenge porn music video which strips my body naked. Now Scooter has stripped me of my life's work, that I wasn't given an opportunity to buy. Essentially, my musical legacy is about to lie in the hands of someone who tried to dismantle it.

This is my worst case scenario. This is what happens when you sign a deal at fifteen to someone for whom the term 'loyalty' is clearly just a contractual concept. And when that man says 'Music has value', he means its value is beholden to men who had no part in creating it.

When I left my masters in Scott's hands, I made peace

with the fact that eventually he would sell them. Never in my worst nightmares did I imagine the buyer would be Scooter.

For those who need a lesson in how to emotionally manipulate teenage girls and the court of public opinion, look no further than this.

Only Taylor Swift could make being one of the most successful female singers of all time, with eyewatering financial success and extreme parental and music industry support, sound like a hardship. She "pleaded," she made "excruciating choices," she "made peace." But music that she "wrote on my bedroom floor," music that she "dreamed up," music for which she signed a "deal at fifteen to someone for whom the term 'loyalty' is clearly just a contractual concept," is now owned by someone who is a "worst nightmare," whom she cried about. Both of these men controlled her, manipulated her, exploited her! Bring them down! Overthrow the patriarchy! #IStandWithTaylor! You get the message.

As if this wasn't enough, Swift then released a follow-up a few months later in which, despite months of behind-the-scenes wrangling, Swift accused both Braun and Borchetta of stopping her from playing her old hits at the American Music Awards. In another highly emotionally charged post on social media, Swift details how, in her eyes, she has been forbidden from rerecording or playing her old music.

Swift, under the heading "Don't know what else to do," published a tweet that stated the following (I removed some of the post due to its length but included the essential parts):

Guys—It's been announced recently that the American Music Awards will be honoring me with the Artist of the Decade Award at this year's ceremony. I've been planning to perform a medley of my hits throughout the decade on the show. Scott Borchetta and Scooter Braun have now said that I'm not allowed to perform my old songs on television because they claim that would be re-recording my music before I'm allowed to next year. Additionally—and this isn't the way I had planned on telling you this news—Netflix has created a documentary about my life for the past few years. Scott and Scooter have declined the use of my older music or performance footage for this project, even though there is no mention of either of them or Big Machine Records anywhere in the film.

I feel very strongly that sharing what is happening to me could change the awareness level for other artists and potentially help them avoid a similar fate. The message being sent to me is very clear. Basically, be a good little girl and shut up. Or you'll be punished. This is WRONG. Neither of these men had a hand in the writing of those songs. They did nothing to create the relationship I have with my fans. So this is where I'm asking for your help. Please let Scott Borchetta and Scooter Braun know how you feel about this. Scooter also manages several artists who I really believe care about other artists and their work. Please ask them for help with this—I'm hoping that maybe they can talk some sense into the men who are exercising tyrannical control over someone who just wants to play the music she wrote.[154]

Everything about this appeal to her fanbase is despicable. Even the title "Don't know what else to do" is absurd. You don't know what else to do? Working it out via normal contract negotiations would be a start. Second, don't try and emotionally manipulate your fanbase to ruin people's lives using words and phrases such as *tyrannical, WRONG, be a good little girl and shut up.* Her appeal is that she's *only* doing this for other artists. Help me so I can help other artists! I just want to play my own music!

A spell is cast.

To the legion of adoring teenage fans who treat the ground Swift walks on as hallowed, this was a declaration of war. Forget the traditional methods of battle, this was a cruise missile to the heart of the "Swifties," those young girls who saw Taylor as the reincarnation of Joan of Arc, the fearless French saint taking charge against the marauding English. Cue Swiftie D-Day. Within days, Scooter Braun was receiving death threats. "I came home tonight to find my wife had received a phone call threatening the safety of our children ... I am at a loss."[155] Both Braun and Borchetta had doxing threats afterward. Four years later, Braun claims he is *still* intimidated by these threats.

Swift's emotional manipulation of her fanbase to achieve her desired outcome is toxic femininity on display. Emotionally charged language, portraying Swift as some kind of child prodigy exploited by wicked men, is a symptom, not of the patriarchy, but of the matriarchy in which we live. Swift's parents, who did everything to exploit her talent and success, went in with eyes wide open to the deal with Big Machine when she was fifteen. But their daughter believes a different set of rules ought to apply to her versus everyone else.

Taylor Swift follows the rule of modern feminism, which means she can concoct fiction and expect the world to accept it as truth. She knows that if she screams the feminist lie loud enough, the truth won't matter when it is finally exposed.

In June 2023, the press broke the news that not only did Swift's father know about the sale of her music from Big Machine to Ithaca, but he made $15 million from the deal.[156] This makes sense since, as we previously noted, Scott Swift was a 5 percent shareholder in Big Machine, and there were *only* five shareholders. Braun also offered Taylor the chance to buy her catalog several times. Messages, emails, shareholder details. All of these facts defeat Swift's "innocent schoolgirl" narrative—but not in the court of public opinion where she reigns supreme. So, instead, Braun and Borchetta were figuratively hit by the Swiftie school bus. To add further insult to injury, Braun sold the catalog of Swift's prerecorded records a year after he purchased them, but he continues to receive death threats and hate from her fanbase to this day.

John Mayer was correct. Neither he, nor any of the men who have endured abuse due to a narrative spun by an adult woman who has a penchant for fantasy, have deserved it. And now it isn't just "cheap songwriting" that Taylor Swift engages in—rather, it's costly, underhanded business tactics that result in real-life death threats. What she engages in is

MAKE HIM A SANDWICH

what I refer to as toxic femininity. Women are now harnessing feminine guile and beauty to exploit the rich mines of public outrage for commercial success. It's as deceptive as it is evil. It should be mentioned here that Swift went on to rerecord her old back catalog, earning even more money for herself while also still collecting extraordinary royalties from her pre-existent records despite their new ownership.

Hocus pocus.

PATRIARCHY

There was a well-known experiment, allegedly carried out by the CIA, in which eighteen people were placed in a room, seventeen of whom were CIA agents and one who was an unwitting member of the public. The person running the experiment showed everyone in the room a picture of a triangle and asked each person, one after the other, to simply state what they saw. Despite it clearly being a triangle, all the agents were instructed to instead say they saw a square. When the instructor at last called upon the member of the public to describe what he saw, he too said a square. What this psychological experiment reveals, among many other things, is that repetition works.

If society routinely insists that the patriarchy exists,

despite overwhelming evidence to the contrary, eventually people will stop believing their own eyes.

The academic establishment has aggressively pushed the narrative that we live, breathe, and operate in a patriarchy that actively suppresses the rights of women. In a 2012 article in *The Atlantic*, University of Maryland sociology professor Philip Cohen wrote a piece headlined "America Is Still a Patriarchy."[157] In the article, Cohen (who seems to enjoy the accolade of being part of the "feminist academic establishment") writes:

> *In fact—my interpretation of the facts—the United States, like every society in the world, remains a patriarchy: they are ruled by men. That is not just because every country (except Rwanda) has a majority-male national parliament, and it is despite the handful of countries with women heads of state. It is a systemic characteristic that combines dynamics at the level of the family, the economy, the culture and the political arena.*

Similarly, in a 2022 interview, Harvard Kennedy School faculty members Erica Chenoweth and Zoe Marks also attested to the rise of patriarchy in the United States. In a call to urgent action, Chenoweth asserts that "Americans who are interested in protecting and improving democracy in the United States must see these assaults on women's equality as assaults on democracy."[158]

She claims there is a rise of autocracy in the United States as well as in countries like Turkey, Russia, and Hong Kong. As just one example of this alleged rise, she names the elimination of drive-through voting as a hardship experienced by female voters. Because, apparently, everybody ought to know that females struggle to get out of cars. Elsewhere, she describes the "full-out assaults of the rights of trans children" as inextricably linked to women's rights.[159] Of course, she is never tasked with having to actually make sense of her claims. These sorts of entirely nonacademic arguments being made by academia routinely go unchallenged, because ... feminism.

It has been said that if people desire to know who rules over them, they need but identify whom they are not allowed to criticize. One might imagine that if we did live under patriarchal-autocratic rule, these women (who seem to never shut up) wouldn't be given so much free reign to keep publicly attacking men. On the flip side, if the male faculty at Harvard got together to produce article after article critical of women, we'd expect those men to be formally condemned, socially ostracized, and to likely lose their careers. What does this signal about the true nature of Western society?

The idea that we are living under a patriarchy truly begs belief.

In the United States, women surpass men in terms of college degrees—39.1 percent compared with just 36.6 percent in 2021. In that same year, men committed suicide 3.9 times more than women,[160] and women lived on average five years longer than men.[161] Women also hold more jobs in the workforce altogether and hold more managerial positions than their male peers.[162]

From a legislative perspective, it is obviously idiocy to say we live in a patriarchy. It is quite literally *illegal* to discriminate against someone on the basis of gender, religion, or sexual identity. Ironically, just as the rhetoric around the patriarchy grows more hysterical, women are occupying more and more senior positions in the government, academia, and business. Women are in ascendency all over the Western world. There are female presidents and prime ministers, board members, and executives.

Which leads me to what the reality is of our current state of play: We aren't living under a patriarchy—but rather, a matriarchy. An intentional and deceptive matriarchy which is hell-bent on convincing the public not to believe its own eyes. The diversionary tactic employed is to have women shriek about the patriarchy, so no one notices the matriarchy which surrounds it.

It is women who now dominate the cultural and political conversation. And since the dawn of the #MeToo era, those women cannot be meaningfully challenged. The frankly bizarre cultural insistence to simply "believe women" is now a base assumption perpetuated by the media, politicians, and, of course, the feminist lobby.

Yet, this is just the latest tide in the rise of the matriarchy. In an article titled "Beware the Matriarchy" published in 2021 for *The American Conservative*, contributing editor Carmel Richardson writes:

> *The feminization of higher education says as much about women as it does about men, who now make up just 40 percent of college students and account for 71 percent of the decline in enrollment in higher education over the last five years. At this rate, men are but a few years from earning one college degree for every two women who graduate…Politics compounds the statistics as, unsurprisingly, colleges have little interest in vocally championing men in our post-feminist political consciousness.*[163]

Once you control the classroom and the legislative agenda,

the rest should flow easily downstream. Richardson cites an article written by Hanna Rosin in *The Atlantic*, where Rosin astonishingly puts forth the question as to whether a modern economy is not better suited to women altogether—whether, instead of men, women should just be the *de facto* leaders. She writes that "the attributes that are most valuable today—social intelligence, open communication, the ability to sit still and focus—are, at a minimum, not predominantly male."[164] The female superpowers of empathy and understanding have been hijacked, twisted, and coopted into advancing the liberal agenda. Now we're told to believe that anything that aspires to the masculine, anything which appeals to innate manhood, is wrong—simply because it isn't the female.

Still don't believe me? Ask yourself a simple question: When is anything male allowed to be applauded without the accusation of "toxic masculinity"? Take it further than that: When is International Men's Day? Why do businesses not put "male owned" on the side of their packaging like they do with "women owned"? Why does breast cancer receive so much more attention than prostate cancer? Why are gender equity rankings always ranked to talk about women and not the inverse? Why do governments have departments talking about women but none about men?

The age of the matriarchy is fully upon us.

BEHIND EVERY CRAZY
WOMAN (NINE RULES)

I graduated from high school in 2007 and enrolled immediately at the University of Rhode Island for my undergraduate studies. Like most people, the years that I spent tucked away on a college campus were years I spent learning about who I was outside the purview of my parents. It was a time for exploration and experimentation, an opportunity to be "truly free."

Somewhere on that misty New England campus, I was first introduced to the concept of feminism which was broadly defined by my professors and peers as "women supporting other women against the ever-present claws of the patriarchy."

The patriarchy (also loosely defined by professors and peers) was the ever-present, male-dominated organization of our society, which, at every layer, sought to intimidate and sub-jugate women. And as an eagle-eyed, college-educated young woman, I found proof of its existence virtually everywhere.

Like the night my friend Lydia cried her eyes out to me in her sorority house because she had given her virginity to a fraternity guy who promised he really loved her but failed to mention the approximate eight other girls he was also really loving. I'll never forget her laughter through the tears as we blasted Taylor Swift's "Picture to Burn" and sang our young hearts out. It turned out it wasn't as easy as a catchy lyric for Lydia to rid herself of her feelings for him. All at once, the feminist message that casual sex or promiscuity could be freeing seemed to conflict with reality. Over the next three years, I watched as she repeatedly returned to that relationship, hoping that he might come to his senses and finally want only her. He never did, but she never stopped trying. I knew why that was. In fact, I had *learned* in a women's studies course that part of the patriarchal structure is the pressure it places on women to fix men. Through early cultural indoctrination, we are imbibed with a responsibility to make men better.

At least, that's what I had learned.

As a newfound feminist (my college drug of choice), I saw it as my responsibility to stand by my girlfriend and inch her away from her patriarchal inclinations. Together, we could come to recognize our full potential by baptizing ourselves in feminist scripture. *We didn't need men to define our worth! In fact, the very pursuit of men was evidence of our submission to dated, societal ideals.*

We were never more inspired than on a girl's night, conversing while drinking Red Bull vodkas and trashing the existence of men.

"Behind every crazy woman is a man that made her that way" offered one of my close friends as we laughed and slid into another alcohol-induced state of indifference. It was a quotation I've never forgotten.

At the time, I thought it to be brilliant, funny, and ever so true. It substantiated my women's studies professor's teaching that women who take control over their lives are often deemed crazy. She emphasized that when women do the right thing and stand up for themselves, they are unjustly dismissed as mental. Men, she pointed out, no matter how horrendous their actions, are hardly ever perceived as emotionally unstable. It was necessary, then, for us to become "unapologetically crazy" in order to break free from the design of the patriarchy. Thus, I began to envy and befriend women who had an uninhibited approach to their lives and relationships.

There was Allison, a girl I met in a journalism class who maintained three boyfriends, simultaneously, none of whom ever discovered her infidelity. I was fascinated by her and the exceeding effort it took to maintain her duplicitous lifestyle. She would often visit sex stores and spoke to me in detail about her many lewd purchases. She lectured me repeatedly about the outdated concept of monogamy and insisted that men shouldn't be the only ones allowed to have fun.

Then there was Joanne, another fellow classmate with a radically different approach. Joanne very much believed in monogamy and had met her someone special during her freshman year. She knew he was someone special because he understood she was not going to be a traditional female. More specifically, she had trained him to never desire sex and to recognize that it was never going to be her place to cook or clean for him. She refused to ever wear makeup and rarely ever wore anything other than sweatpants and sweatshirts. And as a matter of protest, she refused to exercise. She told me that if a man truly loved someone, he must rinse himself of any expectations. And I guess he truly loved her because he stayed around.

But there was no person in all of my years at university

who provided me with more educational entertainment than Alexandra. Standing at 5 feet 8 inches, with long, dark brown hair and olive skin, Alex was two years my senior, and, by every meaningful objective standard a stunning beauty. Evidently, not even beauty could topple the patriarchy as she, too, suffered at the hands of a serial cheater. Her good looks outdone only by her inherent brilliance, Alex did not take the disrespect lightly. She was never interested in singing away her pain with a Taylor Swift song. Rather, each time she phoned me, it signaled the start of an adventure.

Drive-bys were standard. She'd pick me up in her car, and we'd circle the block near her boyfriend's rental to see if his car was there. Then she'd text him and ask him what he was up to to see if he dared to lie. And he always dared—texting back that he was "home, just chillin'" when the empty driveway told a different tale.

Most impressive were her digital spy capabilities. She had successfully figured out all of his university passwords, which came in handy when she wanted to enact revenge upon him for his infidelities. She'd unregister him for classes, send crude emails from his accounts, and sign him up for various gay porn websites and affiliations.

She would regularly check his social media accounts to see which women he was corresponding with in private. As a preventative measure (and without his knowledge), she would routinely block women she came across whom she suspected, based on their appearance, he might be interested in.

The toxicity of their relationship peaked one summer when she discovered he was (once again) having a months-long affair with a young woman from a nearby university. This time, Alexandra wanted to make him really suffer. Armed with a spare key to his summer rental, Alexandra waited until both he and his roommates were out at a game and then let herself into their rental. She made a beeline to his bedroom in pursuit of his beloved sneaker collection.

Alexandra's boyfriend spent a lot of time and money researching and collecting sneakers. Some were signed by his favorite athletes while others were limited editions he sometimes traded or swapped. He went to great lengths to keep his collection neat, painstakingly organizing each pair within their original boxes inside his closet.

I was back in my home state when I received her phone call. "I just threw his sneakers off the Newport Bridge. I took just one of each pair and threw them off the bridge."

I broke into hysterical laughter. What she had done was clearly outrageous but unquestioningly genius. I pictured her boyfriend coming home to discover that exactly one of each of his shoes was missing. It was somehow so much worse than if she had just resolved to dump all of the pairs. It would bring him real psychological suffering because he would have to eventually bring himself to throw out all of the other halves.

I laughed for weeks considering his one-shoe predicament. Though not present in the plot or execution, I was admittedly a never-ending source of affirmation for Alexandra as she rationalized her every move.

To the untrained eye, what she had done might have seemed a bit crazy, but the feminist I was becoming understood her actions to be completely acceptable and well within reason given the suffering she was made to endure at the whims of another gluttonous man.

I was certain that my women's studies professor would cheer her on. She'd say something about taking back our power and ignoring a society that seeks to reframe and diagnose our humanity by constraining our every impulse.

This was Candace Owens in early adulthood—learning to throw caution to the wind.

As I sit here, ten years removed from my college days, I reflect with increasing astonishment over the utter nonsense of my earlier ideas. I find myself frustrated at the institutionalization of modern feminism, with its race-to-the-bottom doctrine masquerading as a movement.

Modern feminism is a parasite. It has no real definition or goal and is without any purpose beyond cultural obsoletion. And like all parasites, it eats through life, and, if not stopped, it will eventually destroys its host.

When I think back to my many conversations with Allison, Joanne, and Alexandra, I see four eager hosts lured by a concept of undoing.

Allison wanted to undo monogamy ... until she didn't. Until her three boyfriends turned into just one boyfriend who wound up getting another girl pregnant. Until she graduated college and wanted relationships with more meaning that were no longer as readily available to her.

Joanne wanted to undo gender assumptions in her relationship ... until she couldn't. Until she got pregnant a few years after school and her growing belly forced her to recognize biological predispositions. Until the face of her newborn infant girl made her want to stay home and spend every waking second giving motherhood her all.

Alexandra wanted to fight until there was truly nothing left to fight for anymore. Until cops were called, restraining orders were filed, and she learned that restraining her every impulse wasn't a symbol of the patriarchy but of adulthood.

And me, the fourth host? I was arguably the worst among them because I was cheering them on. I was the dedicated audience laughing and applauding their every move. Never once did I attempt to reason or dissuade. I imagined myself to be something of an amphitheater, amplifying drama to the masses.

It is only today, and with the utmost clarity that only hindsight can provide, that I now recognize my previous insanity.

In fact, far from the idea that behind every crazy woman is a man who made her that way, the truth is that behind every crazy woman is another crazy woman egging her on.

It's the woman in the comment section telling Lena Dunham she looks amazing when she so evidently does not. It's the female journalist inexplicably applauding Kim Kardashian as she ruthlessly mauls a teenager online for daring to ask if she might have something more to offer than her nude body. It's the flood of women clapping like seals when another toxic term like *body positivity* is passed around to the detriment of young women everywhere.

Modern feminism has conditioned women to lie. To lie repeatedly and senselessly to one another—and perhaps worst of all—to lie to ourselves.

Look around. Look at the women whom the world chooses to elevate and encourages other women to emulate. Ask yourself if outside of the money they earn that may afford them certain privileges—do you truly believe these women are happy? Don't allow their routine displays of monetary wealth distract you from noticing the spiritual bankruptcy they suffer.

Now, look at the women pop culture chooses to ignore. The women who don't cling to feminism as a deity. The women who embody wholesomeness, centering their lives on family and real faith. These women are often castigated as being "close-minded" or "internalized misogynists." They are quietly confident and exude a truer beauty, comfort, and happiness. They are in equal parts hated and ignored by the mainstream media in a manner so senseless that it only works to underscore an age-old truth: Misery loves company. The rabid feminist who attempts to persuade the public against the traditional lifestyle sees within it her own personal shortcomings.

A life led believing in permanent class struggle—men versus women, fat versus thin, rich versus poor—is a life mired by unhappiness.

The history of the feminist movement teaches us that crazy women have and will continue to egg on other crazy women. Radical women will inspire the next generation to crave even more radicalism. Whatever the fight of yesterday, there is always another fight to look to in the future. And, of course, it will be deemed just as urgent and necessary as the one before. One hundred years ago, we were fighting for the right of women to vote. Today, we focus our efforts to ensure that women on a tennis court are paid the same as men even when they play less games and sets. Because … equality! Don't think—just fight the new and never-ending fight.

And the next one after that.

Real women don't need fake feminism, for it is an unceasing struggle. Now, quite removed from my college days, my new mantra is that behind every happy woman is a woman who simply told her the truth. The truth is that modern feminists are disciples of chaos, and chaos does not render someone freer.

And to that end, I now present, conclusively, my nine true rules for women.

RULE #1: BE BEAUTIFUL

Great men throughout history have illogically risked duty, power, and even death for beautiful women. Adam relinquished a perfect paradise for the desires of Eve. Epics recorded from the ancient world drive home the universal theme that men are driven by beautiful women. Helen, deemed to be the most beautiful woman in the world, inspired the fall of the great Trojan Empire. When she runs away from her king, he raises an army to regain her, and after a decade of war, bloodshed, and great warriors lost, the great city of Troy collapsed. Cleopatra and Mark Antony—a dramatic historic account of love, war, defeat, and suicide. Entire armies of men have gone to war and toppled over the pursuit of a woman. In more modern times, we have watched men work their entire lives to put themselves into positions of power, only to fall due to their private dealings with women. The lesson is that a woman's beauty is a natural gift: It stirs a desire within men that shatters all else. Trends encouraging women to be fat and find virtue in vulgarity are those that strip women of inherent power. Do not relinquish your magic.

Also, recognize that beauty belongs to nature. It is natural beauty that should be aspirational. Aging is also of nature and therefore a thing of beauty. Wisdom is a thing of beauty. Those who fight beyond reason to hold on to their youth inevitably wind up appearing deformed and unwise.

RULE #2: KEEP YOUR MYSTERY

To that same end, remember that beauty is in part mystery. Men are drawn by what they see but even further by what they don't know. There is an element of wonder to woman-hood—a natural curiosity it elicits. The natural phenomenon of womanhood has been grossly deteriorated by social media,

MAKE HIM A SANDWICH

where overexposure (whether physical or mental) garners the most clicks. That feedback loop creates narcissism and selfishness. Selfishness runs counter to femininity. A man wants to work to know a woman and to feel that he has earned the reward of her love and selflessness.

RULE #3: HAVE SOME SHAME

There is no one on Earth who isn't facing some sort of personal battle. There is also no person on earth who triumphed any personal battle by sharing it with strangers on the web. Oversharing does not make women braver. Recognize that those who engage in this online feminist fad do so out of a lack of personal stability and a desire to fill a void with voyeuristic internet "likes." The temporary high provided from strangers issuing throwaway compliments will quickly fade. Quit treating social media like your personal shrink. Instead, seek to build a real-world community of family and friends to share yourself with.

RULE #4: EXERCISE COMPASSION, BUT WITH CAUTION

Women are biologically wired to feel bad. We are more

emotional than men, and that is hardly anything worth arguing about because it's a good thing. I believe that our emotions were intended to serve our families, to rear our young, to take care of our old, to support our immediate communities. Feminism created an opportunity for our government to hack our emotions to our own detriment. We demanded work and more governance to raise our young, the results of which have produced various societal ills. When the government wishes to pass legislation, they simply figure out how to make women feel upset about the issue.

Open borders make women feel bad by opining about migrants and claiming they are just impoverished people who want an opportunity.

Transgenderism makes women feel bad about cross-dressing men by making a spurious claim that more children will commit suicide unless they perpetuate this ideology.

The *Department of Education* makes women feel badly about the fact they are not leading the same lives as men. Government will then be able to collect taxes from every working person in society, plus enjoy the benefit of implanting the ideas that benefit the government in their children's mind.

The list goes on. Since women won the right to vote, it seems that government has managed to grow itself tenfold by making emotional arguments rather than logical ones. It's a matter of import that women learn to recognize when they are being emotionally manipulated. Do not abandon compassion but exercise it with caution. When feeling emotional, pause and think about who or what benefits the most from your emotions. If the answer isn't "me, my family, and/or my community," then consider why that may be.

RULE #5: STOP LYING

Every time you tell a lie, you render yourself and the person you tell the lie to weaker. Women should be less concerned with *feeling* bad and more concerned with *doing* bad. Don't look at a man wearing a dress and tell him he is a woman. Lies are an infectious disease. Tell enough of them, and they will eventually infect the society you live in terminally.

RULE #6: LEAN OUT

In 2013, Facebook's chief operating officer Sheryl Sandberg wrote a bestselling book titled *Lean In*. Within its pages, she encourages women to lean in to their career ambitions. Her book is an ode to the working professional, further illustrating how a woman can "have it all" despite societal double standards. Sandberg even writes about her and her husband's concept of a "peer marriage," one in which they treat each other like business partners as they tackle parenting.

Instead, I would like to encourage women to lean out. Accept that no, you cannot do it all, and then ask yourself: Why on earth would any person want to? Lean out of the frustration of trying to prove your worth to the worthless ideals of feminism. With few exceptions, women are not particularly suited to the grueling, day-to-day environment of climbing a corporate ladder, and that's okay. Male strength does not signify female weakness any more than female strength signifies male weakness. The sexes are different but complementary to each other. Trying to excel at things that don't come naturally to you will not make you happy.

RULE #7: LET HIM LEAD

Recognize the yin and yang. When a woman fully embraces the feminine and allows a man to embrace the masculine, a balanced union is formed. Ignore the feminist doctrinal points that pervert a man's desire to lead as a sexist inclination. Rather, his desire to lead is an innate desire to protect what he deems to be of value. Allow him to put himself through stress and risk so he can serve his family in the way that he is biologically inclined to.

RULE #8: UNLEASH THE MAMA BEAR

There is nothing more aspirational than becoming a mother. Motherhood unlocks within a woman a purpose that transcends all others. Women will never feel more certain of their inherent strength and ability than when it comes to rearing children. There is no task more equal parts challenging and rewarding. Raising children is the most crucial responsibility in the world.

RULE #9: MAKE HIM A SANDWICH

I think back to Cardi B and the Twitter exchange that began it all—a woman who had found fame and fortune and was mocking me publicly for daring to make my husband a sandwich. Having attached herself to the feminist principle that nudity equates to power, she undoubtedly meant it when she said that my conservative position in a kitchen serving my family was sending women back. She probably never considered that "sending women back" is very much my intent. I am nostalgic for the demure. I long for a society where the housewife is heralded as the hero that she is. Raising children to be productive members of society is the toughest job in the world.

Unfortunately for Cardi B, rapping explicitly about her lady parts did not further the sanctity of her marriage. Her feminist willingness to share the most intimate parts of her body with the world did not make her husband respect her more. In December 2019, a woman came forward to reveal she had been having an affair with Cardi's husband while Cardi was pregnant with their first child. Shortly thereafter, in 2020, she filed for divorce but withdrew her petition a few months later in an apparent effort to fight for their family. Rumors of infidelity continued to plague the couple with multiple women similarly claiming that her husband, Offset, had been unfaithful. In December 2023, Cardi had a public breakdown on social media. Through tears, she accused her husband of continually choosing to play games with her when she was at her most vulnerable. With her voice breaking, she charged that Offset had treated her "dirty" throughout the years despite all she had done for him. Shortly thereafter, Cardi confirmed that she was single and no longer interested in determining whether or not Offset had been unfaithful.

My heart genuinely broke for her. Hearing any woman

in a state of pain over their family is naturally devastating. And despite our very many differences, I have always maintained that there is much to admire about Cardi B. She came from nothing and made something of herself. A former gang member and stripper, the odds were implausibly stacked against her, and yet she managed to break away from those lifestyles, earning herself an audience due to her personality. But rather than appreciating the fact that she defied statistics, Hollywood convinced her that in order to say relevant, she had to defy the norm, setting her upon a never-ending quest to shock and surprise. Cardi's tears on Instagram proved that despite the many awards, despite the magazine covers and feminist applause, despite having earned millions—she still wasn't happy. Why?

Because money and attention amount to nothing in the grand scheme of what makes a woman feel whole. And though she may never admit it, I believe that what Cardi craves is tradition. A happy home led by a husband who gives her the confidence to know she is enough.

Feminists took the act of a woman making a sandwich in a kitchen and transformed it into a mascot for female oppression. I would like to reclaim it. I'm calling for a revolution against the revolution. I'm calling on women to buck the trend of leaning into a corporate ladder in an effort to prove a zero-sum, feminist point. The point should be happiness.

If I have learned anything in the pursuit of happiness, it's that traditions work, motherhood is aspirational, and home is in fact where the heart is.

So for the love of God and all things holy, make him a sandwich.

NOTES

INTRODUCTION

1   Paraphrased with emphasis added from Confucian source #19 Yue Ji / "Record of Music" chapter of the *Book of Rites*, https://ia801805.us.archive.org/25/items/ApolloHumanRights-Books/57593829-Li-Ji-Legge.pdf, p. 271.

2   Kenneth Garger, "Biden Removes Mention of Dr. Seuss from Read Across America Day," *New York Post*, March 2, 2021, https://nypost.com/2021/03/02/biden-removes-mention-of-dr-seuss-from-read-across-america-day/.

3   Ashley Collman, "Candace Owens and Tucker Carlson Spent Nearly 5 Minutes Slamming Cardi B's Performance of 'WAP' at the Grammys, claiming it's destroying America," *Business Insider*, March 16, 2021, https://www.businessinsider.com/tucker-carlson-candace-owens-attack-cardi-b-wap-grammys-performance-2021-3?utm.

1: BIOLOGY

4   Spencer Klavan, "Be a Man," *The American Mind*, November 6, 2019, https://americanmind.org/salvo/be-a-man/.

5   Klavan, "Be a Man."

6   Edward O. Wilson, *On Human Nature* (Harvard University Press, 2004), 124.

7   Ibid., 125.

8   Ibid., 124.

9   Ibid., 123.

10   Ibid., 127.

11   Ibid., 132.

12   Shir Adani and Maja Cepanec, "Sex Differences in Early Communication Development: Behavioral and Neurobiological Indicators of More Vulnerable Communication System Development in Boys," Croatian Medical Journal 60, no. 2 (2019): 141-149, (doi). 10.3325/cmj.2019.60.141. PMID: 31044585; PMCID: PMC6509633.

13   Kashmira Gander, "Children's Muscles Recover Faster from Exercise than Endurance Athletes, New Research Suggests," *Newsweek*, April 24, 2018, https://www.newsweek.com/childrens-muscles-recover-faster-exercise-endurance-athletes-new-research-897829.

14   Maressa Brown, "Lance Bass Says It Was 'Hard Not to Get Discouraged' During His 'Difficult' Surrogacy Journey: 'Am I Being Told That I Should Not Have Kids?'" *yahoo!life*, May 28, 2023, https://www.yahoo.com/lifestyle/lance-bass-twins-ivf-surrogacy-challenges-144548443.html?mibextid=Zxz2cZ&guccounter=1.

15   Megyn Kelly, "Megyn Kelly Explains Why She Will No Longer Use 'Preferred Pronouns' as Trans Ideology Grows," *The Megan Kelly Show*, June 2, 2023, YouTube Video, https://www.youtube.com/watch?v=FxB0LHvS4fg.

16   Matt Walsh (@MattWalshBlog), "A heartfelt message to Dylan Mulvaney," Twitter, February 14, 2023, https://x.com/MattWalshBlog/status/1625617441219813409.

17   Michelle Toh, "Bud Light Controversy Cost Parent Company about $395 Million in Lost US Sales," *CNN Business*, August 3, 2023, https://www.cnn.com/2023/08/03/business/anheuser-busch-revenue-bud-light-intl-hnk/index.html.

18   Matt Walsh, "A Trans 'Mother' Debates Matt Walsh on Womanhood," *Young America's Foundation Live*, April 6, 2023, YouTube Video, https://www.youtube.com/watch?v=VgXPd-iOu18.

19   Ibid.

20   Wilson, 21–23.

2: DEPARTMENT OF NON-EDUCATION

21   Gloria Steinem, "50 Years Ago, Gloria Steinem Wrote an Essay for Time About Her Hopes for Women's Futures. Here's What She'd Add Today," *Time*, March 5, 2020, https://time.com/5795657/gloria-steinem-womens-liberation-progress/.

22   Steinem, "50 Years Ago, Gloria Steinem Wrote an Essay for Time About Her Hopes for Women's Futures. Here's What She'd Add Today."

23   Jimmy Carter, "Department of Education Organization Act Statement on Signing S. 210 into Law," *The American Presidency Project*, https://www.presidency.ucsb.edu/documents/department-education-organization-act-statement-signing-s-210-into-law.

24   *The Common School Journal*, 3 no. 1 (1841): 15, https://archive.org/details/sim_common-school-journal_1841-01-01_3_1/mode/2up.

25   R.J. Rushdoony, *The Messianic Character of American Education* (Russ House Books, 1995), 29.

26   Rushdoony, *The Messianic Character of American Education*, 31.

27   Dr. Thomas Sowell, *Inside American Education: The Decline, The Deception, The Dogmas* (The Free Press, 1993), 63.

28   Sowell, *Inside American Education*, 63.

29   Christopher Rufo, "The Real Story behind Drag Queen Story Hour," *City Journal*, Autumn 2022, https://www.city-journal.org/article/the-real-story-behind-drag-queen-story-hour.

30   Ibid.

31   Azeen Ghorayshi, "Report Reveals Sharp Rise in Transgender Young People in the U.S.," *The New York Times*, June 10, 2022, https://www.nytimes.com/2022/06/10/science/transgender-teenagers-national-survey.html.

32   Jody L. Herman, Andrew R. Flores, Kathryn K. O'Neil, "How Many Adults And Youth Identify As Transgender In The United States?," *Williams Institute*, June 2022, https://williamsinstitute.law.ucla.edu/wp-content/uploads/Trans-Pop-Update-Jun-2022.pdf

33   Miltra Toossi, "A Century of Change: The U.S. Labor Force, 1950–2050," *Monthly Labor Review*, May 2002, https://www.bls.gov/opub/mlr/2002/05/art2full.pdf.

34   American College of Pediatricians, "The Benefits of the Family Table," February 2021, https://acpeds.org/the-benefits-of-the-family-table/.

35   Ibid.

36   Barbara H. Fiese, PhD, and Marlene Schwartz, PhD, "Reclaiming the Family Table: Mealtimes and Child Health and Wellbeing," *Society for Research in Child Development,* https://files.eric.ed.gov/fulltext/ED521697.pdf.

37   Katherine Schaeffer and Carolina Aragao, "Key Facts about Moms in the U.S.," *Pew Research Center*, May 9, 2023, https://www.pewresearch.org/short-reads/2023/05/09/facts-about-u-s-mothers/.

38   Ibid.

39   Ibid.

40   Ibid.

41   R. Steven Landes, "HB 516 Education, Board of; Policy on Sexually Explicit Instructional Material," *Virginia's Legislative Information System*, https://lis.virginia.gov/cgi-bin/legp604.exe?161+sum+HB516&161+sum+HB516.

42   Terry McAuliffe and Glenn Youngkin, "Virginia Gubernatorial Election Debate," September 28, 2021.

43   Tyler Arnold, "California Teachers Sue over Policy That Forc-

es Them to Hide Students' Gender Preference," *Catholic News Agency*, https://www.catholicnewsagency.com/news/254221/calif-teachers-sue-over-policy-forcing-them-hide-students-gender-preferences-from-parents.

44 Ariel Zilber, "Under Fire Loudoun County School Board Is Hit By Fresh CRT Outrage as Mom Claims Daughter, 6, Was Taught That She Was 'Born Evil Because She Was White' During History Lesson," *Daily Mail*, November 1, 2021, https://www.dailymail.co.uk/news/article-10149109/Loudoun-County-mom-claims-daughter-6-taught-born-evil-shes-white.html.

45 Joshua Q. Nelson, "Virginia Parents Blast School Board over Graphic Books, Critical Race Theory: 'Pretty Despicable,'" *Fox News*, May, 15, 2021, https://www.foxnews.com/us/virginia-parents-loudoun-school-board-graphic-books-critical-race-theory.

46 Michael Ruiz, "Virginia Mom Who Survived Maoist China Eviscerates School Board's Critical Race Theory Push," *Fox5 Washington DC*, June 10, 2021, https://www.fox5dc.com/news/virginia-mom-who-survived-maoist-china-eviscerates-school-boards-critical-race-theory-push.

47 "School Board Recalls," Ballotpedia.org, 2021, https://ballotpedia.org/School_board_recalls#2021.

48 "Fast Facts on Homeschooling," *National Home Education Research Institute*, January 27, 2025, https://www.nheri.org/research-facts-on-homeschooling/.

49 Ibid.

50 Liz Mineo, "A Warning on Homeschooling," *The Harvard Gazette*, May 15, 2020, https://news.harvard.edu/gazette/story/2020/05/law-school-professor-says-there-may-be-a-dark-side-of-homeschooling/.

51 Odette Yousef, "Moms for Liberty among Conservative Groups Named 'Extremist' By Civil Rights Watchdog," *NPR*, June 7, 2023, https://www.npr.org/2023/06/07/1180486760/splc-moms-for-liberty-extremist-group.

52 James Oliphant, "From School Boards to Statehouses, Conserva-

tive Moms for Liberty Push to Grow Influence," *Reuters*, April 6, 2022, https://www.reuters.com/world/us/school-boards-statehouses-conservative-moms-liberty-push-grow-influence-2022-04-06/.

53 Ibid.

54 Yousef, "Moms for Liberty among Conservative Groups Named 'Extremist' By Civil Rights Watchdog."

55 Anne-Claire Bellec, "Mumsnet Increases Personalization for 10 Million Monthly Users with Kameleoon," Kameleoon.com, January 24, 2020, https://www.kameleoon.com/en/blog/mumsnet-kameleoon.

56 "Woman's Hour: The Power List 2013," *BBC*, https://www.bbc.co.uk/programmes/articles/3J92brPmK0hskzhpTV3CrZ0/the-power-list-2013.

57 Justine Roberts, "Let Girls Be Girls Campaign," *mumsnet*, April 17, 2024, https://www.mumsnet.com/articles/let-girls-be-girls.

58 Ibid.

59 Justine Roberts, "Campaign to End Bounty Sales Reps' Access to Maternity Wards—Please Read and Share," *mumsnet*, November 6, 2013, https://www.mumsnet.com/talk/mumsnet_campaigns/1777511-Campaign-to-end-Bounty-sales-reps-access-to-maternity-wards-please-read-and-share.

60 "Marketing on Maternity Wards," UK Parliament, https://edm.parliament.uk/early-day-motion/45812.

61 Letisia Marquez, "Like Mama Bears, Nursing Mothers Defend Babies with a Vengeance," *ScienceDaily*, August 31, 2011, www.sciencedaily.com/releases/2011/08/110830165352.htm.

62 "Female of the Species," by Space, *Spiders*, Gut Records, 1996.

63 Dr. Lynn Rogers, "The Black Bear Mother & Her Cubs," BearWithUs.org, https://bearwithus.org/understanding-bears/the-black-bear-mother-her-cubs/.

64 Olha Omelyanchuk, "Surgeon from the ATO Zone: Before Death, All Soldiers Call for Their Mothers," *Euromaiden Press*, April 8, 2014, https://euromaidanpress.com/2014/08/04/surgeon-from-the-ato-zone-before-death-all-soldiers-call-for-their-mothers/.

3: HAPPILY EVER AFTER

65   Bronnie Ware, "Regrets of the Dying," BronnieWare.com, https://bronnieware.com/blog/regrets-of-the-dying/.

66   Sylvia Ann Hewlett, "Executive Women and the Myth of Having It All," *Harvard Business Review*, April 2002, https://hbr.org/2002/04/executive-women-and-the-myth-of-having-it-all.

67   Genesis 3:17–19, *The Holy Bible*, Revised Standard Version.

68   Betsey Stevenson, Justin Wolfers, "The Paradox of Declining Female Happiness," *NBER Working Paper Series*, https://www.nber.org/system/files/working_papers/w14969/w14969.pdf.

69   Ibid.

70   Ibid.

71   Sian Cain, "Women are happier without children or a spouse, says happiness expert," *The Guardian*, May 25, 2019, https://www.theguardian.com/lifeandstyle/2019/may/25/women-happier-without-children-or-a-spouse-happiness-expert.

72   Andrew Jack and Andrew Hill, "Harvard Fraud Claims Fuel Doubts over Science Of Behaviour," *Financial Times*, June 30, 2023, https://www.ft.com/content/846cc7a5-12ee-4a44-830e-11ad00f224f9?-accessToken=zwAGAOzuk9bgkdOEbMelEu5KRNOD-DhGtAPIk-Q.MEUCIQCBAueVD4_DaXv-7KEKIU-byCTG2kmnwIRo1lDf25Rfx5gIgDAwj3tM7IAiBffEkzA-PI_A6SQ9mkypWrX8K3SSGQ0Tg&sharetype=gift&to-ken=10617e4b-0a57-4731-b54f-1aab4208df7e.

73   Katherine M. Keyes et al., "Is There a Recent Epidemic of Women's Drinking? A Critical Review of National Studies," *National Library of Medicine*, 43, no. 7 (2019), https://www.ncbi.nlm.nih.gov/pmc/articles/PMC6602861/.

74   National Safety Council, "Drug Overdoses," *NSC Injury Facts*, https://injuryfacts.nsc.org/home-and-community/safety-top-ics/drugoverdoses/#:~:text=Few%20opioid%20deaths%20occur%20among,females%20versus%201%2C076%25%20for%20males.

75   "Women and Gambling Related Harm: Research Report"

https://assets.website-files.com/6083d49a695f4ad43b-5148c9/608c0289b6a4806b0c787655_BKM_Women_%26_Gambling_2021_v1.pdf.

76   Christina Hoff Sommers, "6 Feminist Myths That Will Not Die," *Time*, June 17, 2016, https://time.com/3222543/wage-pay-gap-myth-feminism/.

77   "Jordan Peterson's Channel 4 Interview by Cathy Newman - Full Transcript," *Scraps from the Loft*, August 23, 2018, https://scrapsfromtheloft.com/psychology/jordan-petersons-channel-4-interview-cathy-newman-transcript/

78   "World's Billionaires List: The Richest in 2025," edited by Chase Peterson-Withorn, Grace Chung, and Matt Durot, *Forbes*, https://www.forbes.com/billionaires/.

79   World's Billionaires List: Zhou Qunfei, edited by Chase Peterson-Withorn, Grace Chung, and Matt Durot, *Forbes*, https://www.forbes.com/profile/zhou-qunfei/?list=billionaires.

4: BEYOND THE PALE

80   James Crossland, "The Women Who Ended an Emperor," *History Workshop*, April 21, 2021, https://www.historyworkshop.org.uk/violence/the-women-who-ended-an-emperor/.

81   Deborah Hertz, "Dangerous Politics, Dangerous Liaisons: Love and Terror among Jewish Women Radicals in Czarist Russia," *Histoire, économie & société*, 33, no. 4 (2014), https://shs.cairn.info/revue-histoire-economie-et-societe-2014-4-page-94?lang=en.

82   Ibid.

83   Bernard Weinstein and Maurice Wolfthal, *The Jewish Unions in America: Pages of History and Memories* (Open Book Publishers, 2018).

84   "Schaubelt Dead: Haymarket Bomb-Thrower Expires at San Bernardino, Cal.," *True Republican*, October 24, 1896, https://idnc.library.illinois.edu/?a=d&d=STR18961024.2.45&e=------en-20--1--txt-txIN----------.

NOTES

85 Emma Goldman, *Living My Life* (Penguin Classics, 2006).

86 Paul Avrich, *Sasha and Emma: The Anarchist Odyssey of Alexander Berkman and Emma Goldman* (Harvard University Press, 2012), 30–42.

87 Isabella Buzynski, "Jewish Café Culture in New York City," storymaps.com, https://storymaps.arcgis.com/stories/91871ecdb0984ebaabf434c09df708d1.

88 "Q&A: Two New Biographies—Emma Goldman and Margaret Sanger," *Metrofocus*, November 18, 2011, https://www.thirteen.org/metrofocus/2011/11/qa-two-new-biographies-emma-goldman-and-margaret-sanger/.

89 Margaret Sanger, "A Better Race Through Birth Control", *The Thinker*, November, 1923, https://web.archive.org/web/20160501172433/http://www.nyu.edu/projects/sanger/webedition/app/documents/show.php?sangerDoc=306638.xml.

90 Margaret Sanger, "Apostle of Birth Control sees cause gaining here: Hearing in Albany on Bill to Legalize Practice a Milestone in Long Fight of Margaret Sanger—Even China Awakening to Need of Selective Methods, she says," *The New York Times*, April 8, 1923, https://www.nytimes.com/1923/04/08/archives/apostle-of-birth-control-sees-cause-gaining-here-hearing-in-albany.html.

91 Margaret Sanger, "The Eugenic Value of Birth Control Propaganda," *The Birth Control Review*, October 1921, https://bpb-us-e1.wpmucdn.com/blogs.uoregon.edu/dist/7/11428/files/2017/03/Sanger-Eugenic-Value-ve2d9p.pdf.

92 Phoebe, Radical Women's Lives, 1, no. 1, (1989).

5: UGLY, NAKED, AND AFRAID

93 Karensa Cadenas, "Feminism and Flawed Women in Lena Dunham's 'Girls,'" *MS. magazine*, April 14, 2012, https://ms-magazine.com/2012/04/14/flawed-women-and-feminism-in-lena-dunhams-girls/.

94 Claire Danes, "Lena Dunham," *Time*, April 18, 2013, https://time100.time.com/2013/04/18/time-100/slide/lena-dunham/.

95   Mary Harrod, "Girls May Be Flawed, But Its Feminist Legacy Will Last," *The Conversation*, February 10, 2017, https://the-conversation.com/girls-may-be-flawed-but-its-feminist-legacy-will-last-72442.

96   Ibid.

97   Anita Katee, "Lena Dunham poses completely nude outdoors as she says she is a sober, accountable adult who loves being naked," *Daily Mail*, May 29, 2019, https://www.dailymail.co.uk/tvshow-biz/article-7083647/Lena-Dunham-poses-completely-nude-out-doors-says-loves-naked.html.

98   Alice Vincent, "Why the f*** shouldn't women swear?" *The Telegraph*, November 4, 2015, https://www.telegraph.co.uk/women/womens-life/11207309/Why-the-f-shouldnt-women-swear-Lena-Dunham-nails-it.html.

99   Rebecca Mead, "Downtown's Daughter," *The New Yorker*, November 7, 2020, https://www.newyorker.com/magazine/2010/11/15/downtowns-daughter.

100   Sarah Marsh, "Instagram Urged to Crack Down on Eating Disorder Images," *The Guardian*, February 8, 2019, https://www.theguardian.com/technology/2019/feb/08/instagram-urged-to-crack-down-on-ea2ng-disorder- images.

101   "Eating Disorder Statistics," *National Association of Anorexia Nervosa and Associated Disorders*, https://anad.org/eating-disorder-statistic/#general

102   "Data Page: Deaths due to obesity", part of the following publication: Esteban Ortiz-Ospina and Max Roser (2016)—"Global Health," Data adapted from IHME, Global Burden of Disease, retrieved from https://archive.ourworldindata.org/20250825-222531/grapher/deaths-due-to-obesity.html [online resource] (archived on August 25, 2025).

103   "Adult Obesity Facts," *CDC*, May 14, 2024, https://www.cdc.gov/obesity/adult-obesity-facts/?CDC_AAref_Val=https://www.cdc.gov/obesity/data/adult.html.

104   Alyssa Hardy, "Fans React to Tess Holliday's 'Cosmopolitan

UK' Cover," *Teen Vogue*, August 30, 2018, https://www.teen-vogue.com/story/tess-holliday-cosmopolitan-uk-cover.

105 Jordan B Peterson (@jordanbpeterson) Twitter, May 16, 2022, https://twitter.com/jordanbpeterson/status/1526279181545390083.

106 Dani Di Placido, "Jordan Peterson Widely Mocked After Calling Sexy Swimsuit Cover 'Authoritarian,'" *Forbes*, May 18, 2022, https://www.forbes.com/sites/danidiplacido/2022/05/17/jordan-peterson-widely-mocked-aber-calling-sexy- swimsuit-cover-authoritarian/?sh=250d2742ca4a.

107 Lena Dunham, "False Labor," *Harper's Magazine*, December 2020, https://harpers.org/archive/2020/12/false-labor-lena-dunham-fertility/.

108 James Patrick Herman, "Lena Dunham Opens Up About Addiction, Rehab at Friendly House Benefit," *Variety*, October 27, 2019, https://variety.com/2019/scene/news/lena-dunham-addiction-rehab-friendly-house-1203384827/

109 Lena Dunham, "Lena Dunham: Why I Chose Hillary Clinton," *Time*, April 25, 2016, https://time.com/4306966/lena-dunham-hillary-clinton-bernie-sanders/.

110 https://www.vanityfair.com/style/2016/07/lena-dunham-remove-guns-jason-bourne-movies

111 Hilary Weaver, "Lena Dunham Is in Favor of Removing All Guns from Jason Bourne Movie Posters," *Vanity Fair*, July 13, 2016, https://www.thewrap.com/lena-dunham-immigration-international-womens-day-essay/.

6: THE KARDASHIAN SCHOOL OF PLASTIC

112 Natalie Finn, "The End of a Kardashian Era: Inside the Decision to Close DASH and the Expansion of the Family Brand," *E News*, April 20, 2018, https://www.eonline.com/news/928826/the-end-of-a-kardashian-era-inside-the-decision-to-close-dash-and-the-expansion-of-the-family-brand.

113 Ruth Styles, "Kim Kardashian Kept 'Leaked' Sex Tapes in a Nike Shoebox under Her Bed: Ray J Speaks after '14 Years in

the Shadows' to Reveal Second Tape DOES Exist But SHE Has the Only Copy—And Accuses Kardashians of Making Billions from 'Abusing My Name,'" *Daily Mail*, May 4, 2022, https://www.dailymail.co.uk/news/article-10778471/Kim-Kardashian-second-sex-tape-Ray-J-says-hits-claim- planned-leak-it.html.

114   Ibid.

115   Ibid.

116   Rachel Krause, "Kim Kardashian Returns to Her Preferred State of Being: Naked on a Magazine Cover," *Stylecaster*, June 15, 2016, https://stylecaster.com/entertainment/celebrity-news/596852/kim-kardashian-naked-gq-cover.

117   Sophie Hirsh, "Kim Kardashian's Essay about Why She's Not a Feminist Doesn't Make Sense," mashable.com, August 16, 2016, https://mashable.com/article/kim-kardashian-essay-feminism.

118   Ibid.

119   Harper's Bazaar Arabia, "Remember This: Kim Kardashian's Bazaar Cover Shoot Inspired By Her Ultimate Style Muse Cher," *Harper's Bazaar Arabia*, August 30, 2017, https://www.harpers-bazaararabia.com/culture/culture-featured-news/kim-kardashian-west-september-cover-star.

120   Jordana Lipsitz, "Kim K. Wrote an Inspiring Essay About Slut-Shaming," *Bustle*, March 8, 2016, https://www.bustle.com/articles/146764-kim-kardashian-wrote-an-essay-condemning-slut-shaming-its-a-totally-inspiring-read?utm_source=chatgpt.com.

121   Nicholas Rice, "Megan Fox Tells Stylist She Cut a Hole in Her Blue Jumpsuit to 'Have Sex' with Machine Gun Kelly," *People*, May 16, 2022, https://people.com/style/megan-fox-tells-stylist-she-cut-a-hole-in-her-jumpsuit-to-have-sex/.

122   Amy Otto, "Men Did Greater Things When It Was Harder To See Boobs," *The Federalist*, June 23, 2016, https://thefederalist.com/2016/06/23/men-did-greater-things-when-it-was-harder-to-see-boobs/.

123   James McTavish, "Internet Pornography: Some Medical and Spiritual Perspectives," *National Library of Medicine*, June 26,

2020, https://pmc.ncbi.nlm.nih.gov/articles/PMC7551539/.

124   Zane Lowe, "Kanye West: 'Jesus is King' and Iconic Sunday Service," *Apple Music*, October 25, 2019, podcast, https://www.youtube.com/watch?v=QuOCvKvrwI8.

125   Eileen Kelly, "Emily Ratajkowski, Retired Pick-Me Girl, on Therapy, Facetune, & Leaving Her Marriage," *Going Mental with Eileen Kelly*, March 9, 2023, podcast, https://open.spotify.com/episode/6srOkAR6imCLt3q7G4kZvP?si=6b9b5e2c-06ed4455&nd=1&dlsi=91599ca1918f466a.

126   Ellen Peirson-Hagger, "Emily Ratajkowski Interview: "I Used to Think Feminism Was Women Hustling,'" *Forbes*, September 26, 2022, https://www.forbes.com/sites/oliviapeluso/2022/09/26/emily-ratajkowski-tory-burch-on-balancing-30-million- followers-and-their-two-cents/?sh=30b63a9a6cd1.

127   Emily Selleck, "Madonna Slams 'Jealous' 50 Cent for 'Talking Smack' about Her Racy Photos," *PageSix*, December 3, 2021, https://pagesix.com/2021/12/03/madonna-slams-50-cent-for-talking-smack-about-racy-photos/.

128   Ibid.

129   Belinda Luscombe, "Madonna's Face and the Myth of Aging Gracefully," *Time*, February 9, 2023, https://time.com/6253977/madonna-face-grammys-2023/.

130   Wendy Geller, "Madonna Jokes About 'Swelling from Surgery' Following Criticism of Her Appearance at 2023 Grammys," *People*, February 20, 2023, https://people.com/style/madonna-jokes-about-surgery-following-2023-grammys-appearance-criticism/#:~:text=%22Look%20how%20cute%20i%20am%20now%20that%20swelling%20from%20surgery,with%20a%20cheeky%20%22lol.%22.

131   Michael Kaplan, "Since 2008, Madonna Only Dates Guys at Least 28 Years Younger," *PageSix*, September 14, 2022, https://pagesix.com/2022/09/14/since-2008-madonna-only-dates-guys-at-least-28-years-younger/.

132   Ibid.

7: ALONG CAME HANNAH

133   Matt Hargreaves, "Pageants, Plies, and Pork: Tales of Connection on the Ballerina Farm," *Utah Farm Bureau Federation*, December 9, 2021, https://www.utahfarmbureau.org/Article/Pageants-Plies-and-Pork-Tales-of-Connection-on-the-Ballerina-Farm#:~:text=Hannah%20grew%20up%20in%20Springville,her%20schooling%20again%20at%20Juilliard.

134   Megan Agnew, "What Men Really Think About Modern Dating—By My Exes," *The Sunday Times*, April 23, 2023, https://www.thetimes.com/life-style/sex-relationships/article/what-men-really-think-about-modern-dating-by-my-exes-z022g7zdc.

135   Sex and the City, Season 4, Episode 17, "A 'Vogue' Idea."

136   Sex and the City, Season 2, Episode 18, "Ex and the City."

137   Sex and the City, Season 1, Episode 12, "Oh Come All Ye Faithful."

138   Sex and the City, Season 2, Episode 18, "Ex and the City."

139   Sex and the City, Season 6, Part A, Episode 9, "A Woman's Right to Shoes."

140   Sex and the City, Season 5, Episode 8, "I Love a Charade."

141   Michael Patrick King, Sex and the City 2, *HBO Films*, 2010.

142   Leslie M. M. Blume, "Candace Bushnell On Sex, Money, And Sarah Palin," *Huffpost*, October 20, 2008, https://www.huffpost.com/entry/candace-bushnell-on-sex-m_b_127632.

143   Liz Raftery, "Candace Bushnell Files for Divorce, Claims Husband Had Affair: Report," *People*, December 7, 2011, https://people.com/celebrity/candace-bushnell-divorce-husband-has-affair-with-ballerina/

144   Laura Pullman, "Interview: Sex and the City Writer Candace Bushnell on Divorce, Dating and Sex in Her Sixties," *The Times*, July 28, 2019, https://www.thetimes.com/world/us-world/article/interview-sex-and-the-city-writer-candace-bushnell-on-divorce-dating-and-sex-in-her-sixties-kpwj556mv.

145   Megan Agnew, "Meet the Queen of Trad Wives (and Her Eight Children)," *The Sunday Times*, July 20, 2024, https://www.thetimes.com/magazines/the-sunday-times-magazine/ar-

ticle/meet-the-queen-of-the-trad-wives-and-her-eight-children-plfr50cgk.

146   Megan Agnew, "My Day with the Trad Wife Queen and What It Taught Me," *The Sunday Times*, July 29, 2024, https://www. thetimes.com/world/us-world/article/my-day-with-the-trad-wife-queen-and-what-i-really-thought-of-her-qmbmmhkp8.

147   Hannah Neeleman, "What I'm Thinking Now …," *Instagram* post, July 31, 2024, https://www.instagram.com/reel/C-GeB-acSJx2/?utm_source=ig_embed&ig_rid=80b1b232-98b5-497f-a188-bec031dfa8c3.

8: HOCUS POCUS

148   Scarlett Harris, "The Musical 'Wicked' Is As Much About Feminism as It Is About Witches," junked.com, November 4, 2014, https://junkee.com/the-musical-wicked-is-as-much-about-feminism-as-it-is-about-witches/44428.

149   Anne T. Donahue, "'We Are the Weirdos': How Witches Went from Evil Outcasts to Feminist Heroes," *The Guardian*, August 28, 2015, https://www.theguardian.com/film/2015/aug/28/ witches-evil-outcasts-feminist-heroes-pop-culture.

150   C.S. Lewis, *Perelandra* (Scribner, 1944), 108.

151   *Dobbs v. Jackson Women's Health Organization*, No. 19–1392 (2022), https://www.supremecourt.gov/opinions/21pdf/19-1392_6j37.pdf.

152   Sam Frizzel, "Taylor Swift Finally Explains Why She's a Feminist and How Lena Dunham Helped," *Time*, August 23, 2014, https://time.com/3165825/taylor-swift-feminist-lena-dunham/#:~:text="Becoming%20friends%20with%20Lena%20 –%20without,saying%20so%2C"%20Swift%20said.

153   Rolling Stone, "John Mayer: Taylor Swift's 'Dear John' Song 'Humiliated Me,'" *Rolling Stone*, June 6, 2012, https://www. rollingstone.com/music/music-news/john-mayer-taylor-swifts-dear-john-song-humiliated-me-107169/.

154   Taylor Swift (@taylorswift13), "Don't know what else to do," Twitter, November 14, 2019, https://twitter.com/taylorswift13/

status/1195123215657508867/photo/3.

155 https://www.papermag.com/swift-death-threats-scooter-braun-#rebelltitem10.

156 TMZ Staff, "Taylor Swift Dad Reportedly Made $15MIn Scooter Braun Music Sale," *TMZ*, June 15, 2023, https://www.tmz.com/2023/06/15/taylor-swift-dad-scott-music-catalog-sale-scooter-braun/.

157 Philip Cohen, "America Is Still a Patriarchy," *The Atlantic*, November 19, 2012, https://www.theatlantic.com/sexes/archive/2012/11/america-is-still-a-patriarchy/265428/.

158 Nora Delaney, "Autocracy and Patriarchy Are Surging Worldwide—But Women Are Pushing Back," *Harvard Kennedy School*, February 28, 2022, https://www.hks.harvard.edu/faculty-research/policy-topics/gender-race-identity/autocracy-and-patriarchy-are-surging-worldwide.

159 Ibid.

160 "Suicide Statistics," *American Foundation for Suicide Prevention*, https://afsp.org/suicide-statistics/.

161 Robert H. Shmerling, M.D., "Why men often die earlier than women," *Harvard Health Publishing*, June 22, 2020, https://www.health.harvard.edu/blog/why-men-often-die-earlier-than-women-201602199137.

162 Jack Kelly, "Women Now Hold More Jobs Than Men in the U.S. Workforce," *Forbes*, January 13, 2020, https://www.forbes.com/sites/jackkelly/2020/01/13/women-now-hold-more-jobs-than-men/?sh=47dd37208f8a.

163 Carmel Richardson, "Beware the Matriarchy," *The American Conservative*, September 21, 2021, https://www.theamericanconservative.com/beware-the-matriarchy/.

164 Ibid.